Rekindling the Flame

STRATEGIES FOR A VITAL
UNITED METHODISM

William H. Willimon
AND
Robert L. Wilson

ABINGDON PRESS
NASHVILLE

REKINDLING THE FLAME:
STRATEGIES FOR A VITAL UNITED METHODISM

Copyright © 1987 By Abingdon Press

This book is printed on acid-free paper.

Library of Congress Cataloging-in-Publication Data

Willimon, William H.
Rekindling the flame.
1. Church renewal—United Methodist Church (U.S.)
2. United Methodist Church (U.S.) 3. Methodist Church— United States.
I. Wilson, Robert Leroy, 1925– II. Title.
    BX8382.2.W56   1987   287'.6   87-1795

ISBN 0-687-35932-5 (alk. paper)

Scripture quotations in this publication are from the Revised Standard
Version of the Bible, Copyrighted 1946, 1952, © 1971, 1973 by the Division
of Christian Education of the National Council of the Churches of Christ in
the U.S.A., and are used by permission.

MANUFACTURED BY THE PARTHENON PRESS AT
NASHVILLE, TENNESSEE, UNITED STATES OF AMERICA

To Bishop W. Kenneth Goodson,
whose love for The United Methodist Church
inspires hope and assurance

Contents

Preface

Preachers often fail to speak out on controversial issues and keep their sermons safe and comfortable, not because they are afraid of their parishioners' rage, but because they have learned to love their people. Every preacher knows how tough it is to say unpleasant things to beloved people. As United Methodist elders who love our church, we wrote this book, not because we wanted to—for it is tough for us to say unpleasant things to those we love—but because we felt that someone must speak up.

We are convinced that The United Methodist Church faces a crisis unequaled to any since the schism preceding the Civil War. The continued membership decline is the major symptom of this crisis, but the issues are deeper and more complex than the loss of members. In any organization, when things are not going well, there are always those who urge silence, unquestioning loyalty, and the suppression of all criticism. But our church is too important to be allowed to wither if there is some means of giving it new life. In good conscience, we could not remain silent.

This book is based on three assumptions: First, the crisis in the church is much more serious than many people realize. No defenses or alibis can hide the fact that, if we continue in the future as we have in the recent past, our church will no longer be viable and effective. Second, God still has a use, perhaps even a need, for The United Methodist Church. We are confident that the people known as United Methodists continue to be called to witness and to serve, to be a unique manifestation of the universal body of Christ. Third, there are specific steps that will not only contribute to a reversal of the present downward spiral, but will also make the church more faithful and effective. The good news is that our church already is blessed with the structure, the message, and the people to change direction. Action will not be easy, but the alternative of continuing our present course is unthinkable.

In the pages that follow, we shall challenge some of the current assumptions operating in our denomination. Some of our recommendations will challenge the vested interests of powerful groups within our church. We are prayerfully convinced that these honest challenges are needed to encourage healthy dialogue and debate . . . and action.

It is a formidable undertaking to recommend strategies for so vast an institution as The United Methodist Church. We bring to this task broad experience in and wide knowledge of the church. One of us has had a decade and a half as pastor, seminary teacher, and lecturer; the other has had three decades of experience as pastor, teacher, and researcher. We have been privileged to visit in nearly every conference of The United Methodist Church and have studied hundreds of individual congregations. Together, we have written over thirty books, but none of more importance to us and, we believe, to the church than this one.

This book would not have been possible without the encouragement and assistance of a great many people. We are particularly appreciative of our colleagues at Duke University for their insights. A special word of thanks is due Candice Y. Sloan of the J. M. Ormond Center for Research, Planning, and Development, who assisted with the research and preparation of the manuscript.

In his book, *And Are We Yet Alive,* Bishop Richard B. Wilke has vividly demonstrated the crisis within United Methodism, warning that the church is sick unto death. The diagnosis has been made; now corrective action must be taken.

WILLIAM H. WILLIMON
ROBERT L. WILSON
DURHAM, NORTH CAROLINA

Revitalization Is Necessary and Possible

Chapter 1. The most significant fact about the mainline Protestant churches in America in the past two decades has been the drastic decline in membership. This began in the 1960s and has continued to the present. While the rate of decrease has varied from year to year, nothing has reversed the steady downward trend. The drop in membership is a symptom of a deep and complex problem; it is already having an effect on the life and mission of the denominations. If the downward trend continues, the role of these churches in both the religious community and the larger society will be drastically and permanently changed.

Extent of Membership Decline

The Methodist and the Evangelical United Brethren Churches each began to experience a decrease in membership in the 1960s. This was obscured by the optimism engendered by the merger of these two denominations in Dallas in 1968. The details of the merger took a couple of years to be worked out and several more years for the overlapping annual conferences to combine. During the early years, a number of EUB congregations, largely in the Pacific Northwest region, withdrew to form a separate denomination.[1] However, by 1970 The United Methodist Church was in place with a total membership of 10,671,744 and 40,653 organized churches.[2]

The decline, which began in each of the denominations before the merger, has continued. By 1984, the total number of members had decreased to 9,266,853; a loss of 1,404,891, or 13 percent. We had lost members equal to almost twice the number of EUBs who had united with the Methodists in 1968. The United Methodist Church, in the fourteen-year period 1970–1984, lost an average of 1,930 members every week. (This decrease is illustrated in Graph 1, p. 13.).

The downward trend has not yet been reversed. Preliminary figures for 1985 give the lay membership as 9,105,046.[3] During calendar year 1985, the total number decreased by 75,692, or an average loss of 1,455 persons each week. This is the equivalent of closing a church of 207 members every day for one year.

The average attendance at the principal service of worship has also shown a downward trend, although at a somewhat slower rate than the membership decline. There were over 442,000 fewer persons attending worship in 1984 than in 1969, a decrease of 11 percent. (This trend is illustrated in graph 2, p. 14.)

Nor is the picture regarding the number of congregations is encouraging. During the period of 1970-1984, United Methodism closed a total of 2,665 local churches, or an average of slightly under four congregations per week.

An examination of the membership trends of several other mainline denominations for the decade and a half from 1968 to 1983 reveals equally dismal pictures. The Episcopal Church had a membership decline of 17 percent.[4] The decrease in the United Church of Christ was 16 percent.[5] The Christian Church (Disciples of Christ) dropped by 29 percent. The recently created Presbyterian Church (USA), the result of a merger between the United Presbyterian Church in the U. S. A. and the Presbyterian Church in the United States, in 1983 had 25 percent fewer adherents than the combined membership of their component parts a decade and a half earlier.

It is difficult to conceptualize the extent of the membership declines suffered by the mainline churches during the 1970s and early 1980s. Every week these denominations averaged a

Graph 1

UNITED METHODIST MEMBERSHIP 1969–1984

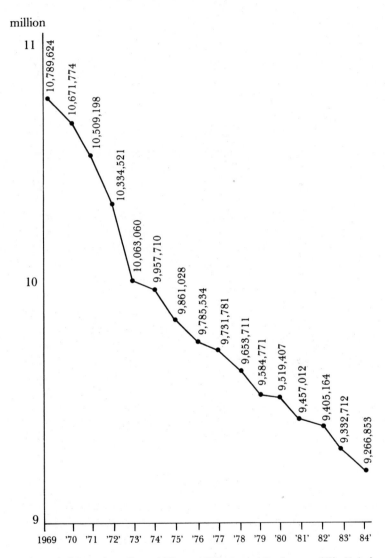

Source of these data: *General Minutes of The Annual Conferences of The United Methodist Church* (General Council on Finance and Administration, Evanston, Illinois), 1969 through 1984 (one figure from each of sixteen volumes).

Graph 2

UNITED METHODIST AVERAGE WORSHIP
ATTENDANCE 1969–1984

million

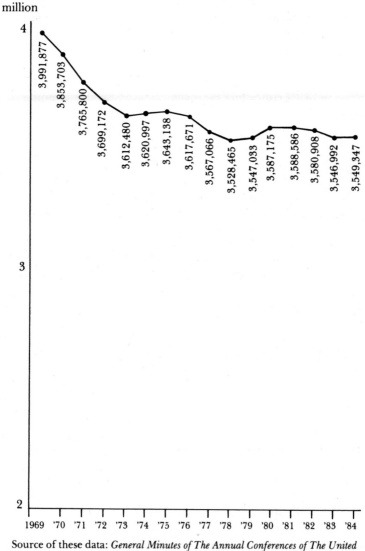

Source of these data: *General Minutes of The Annual Conferences of The United Methodist Church* (General Council on Finance and Administration, Evanston, Illinois), 1969 through 1984 (one figure from each of sixteen volumes).

decline of over five thousand; this is the equivalent of mainline Protestantism's closing one local church of almost seven hundred members every day for a decade and a half.

The significance of this downward trend in membership on these historically prominent denominations and their role in the larger society is great. It may mean a realignment of the religious bodies in America. For example, there are now more members in the Assemblies of God than in the United Church of Christ, a fact that will influence both denominations.

The Impact of the Membership Decline

The long-term decline in membership is already making an impact on the church at both the local and the denominational levels. When a congregation loses members, it is forced to cut back on its program, to reduce staff, to secure a younger and less experienced pastor who receives a lower salary, to delay building maintenance, and to contribute less to the denomination's mission and benevolence programs. Then there are the factors that statistics cannot describe: the grief of seeing one's local church dwindle in size, the sadness when members move elsewhere, and the fear of an increasingly uncertain future. This has been happening in hundreds of congregations, particularly those in the old urban centers. Many of such churches, which once were among the strongest in the denomination, are now struggling to survive.

The membership decrease is affecting our denomination as a whole in several ways. The first is a change in the church's self-image. Methodists have long and correctly considered their church to be one of the major churches in America. For a time it was the largest Protestant group in the nation. There were, of course, the fundamentalist churches and the sectarian groups, but these were perceived to be on the fringes. Such churches were not thought to represent the wave of the future, which was the preserve of Methodism and the other mainline, more liberal denominations.

The continued downward trend is beginning to change

people's image of their church and to contribute to a morale problem, particularly among the clergy. In a society that places a premium on growth, any institution that has declined for two decades is bound to have a serious case of self-doubt. In a religion that believes one of its primary purposes to be to win converts to its Lord and its way of life, the failure to grow may be interpreted as a failure of mission. Church leaders and, increasingly, the people are aware that things are not going well, but are unsure as to what should be done. The majority of our pastors now serve and the majority of our members now live within congregations that appear to have accepted continuous decline as a way of life. Decline is not a way of life, but of death. To live in circumstances of unrelenting, continual decline may cause pastors and laity to accept decline as inevitable.

Despite its decline, The United Methodist Church is still strong. Any organization with a membership in excess of nine million people is hardly insignificant. Nevertheless, the effects of the membership decrease are already evident in the lack of self-confidence, in the pessimism, and in the uncertainty about the church's direction and future.

A second effect of membership loss is a decrease in the influence of the church in the larger society. Methodism has been deeply involved in every reform activity in America, from the anti-slavery campaign of the pre-Civil War period to the civil rights movement of the second half of this century. The twentieth century has been a time in which Methodists have devoted a considerable amount of time, effort, and resources to working for a more humane and just society. A Social Creed to provide guidelines for Methodist Episcopal Church members was adopted in 1906. Several specialized national boards and agencies have been created to deal with such issues as temperance, world peace, race relations, and a variety of other social and economic issues.

The United Methodist Church has continued to take stands on public issues. Its agencies have urged the members to attempt to influence government officials in order to bring about specific social change. However, an organization that is in decline will not command as much attention in the larger society as will one that is growing. A denomination that is unsure of itself will not be able to mobilize its resources to focus on a particular issue. A decrease in new members decreases our contacts with the various ethnic and economic groups within society. Our social commitments wane as we become the church of the aging establishment. The church may continue to raise the ethical and moral issues, but it will have fewer constituents to influence public policy.

A third result of the membership decline is an increased emphasis on institutional maintenance and survival. As a knowledgeable United Methodist leader recently observed, "The church is in a maintenance mode." When an institution feels threatened, its energies flow into self-preservation.

In the local church, self-preservation takes the form of anxiously seeking members. This is illustrated by the lay member's statement, "We simply must recruit some more people, particularly young people, in order to insure that Trinity Church will be here after we are gone." The emphasis was on survival, not mission. The sense of desperation, however, makes the task of securing additonal members more difficult.

In the church's bureaucracy, the emphasis on survival takes the form of extreme defensiveness of the *status quo*. Any questioning of organizational procedures or programs evokes a defensive and negative response. Critics will be labeled as disloyal trouble makers. When leaders are chosen, creativity, courage, and vision will be valued less than loyalty to the *status quo*. The impression is conveyed that the church is an extremely fragile institution that will suffer irreparable damage if even its most loyal supporters raise any questions.

The emphasis on survival at the expense of mission is counter-productive. An air of anxiety does not win persons, but rather causes them to turn away. The church, of all institutions, should know that its purpose is not only to survive, but also to witness and to serve. It should never forget the truth in the admonition, "For whoever would save his life will lose it, and whoever loses his life for my sake will find it" (Matt. 16:25).

A fourth long-term effect of the membership decrease will

be a decrease in income. Despite the decline, total expenditures by The United Methodist Church have increased in the past decade and a half. However, leaner times can be anticipated if the downward trend continues. The income of the church comes largely from the offerings taken in thousands of congregations across the nation. A smaller number of people will ultimately mean a reduced income. Futhermore, the last two decades have seen an increasing number of members moving near the customary retirement period of life, when their incomes tend to be fixed. A large number of our congregations have a relatively high proportion of persons over sixty, with many over seventy years of age. A recent study of a sample of United Methodist congregations revealed that 21.3 percent of church members were age sixty-five and over, compared with 11.5 percent of the total population. Over one third (34.4 percent) of the members are fifty-five and older. In contrast, only 12.4 percent of the church's members are in the nineteen to thirty-four age group, compared to 28.4 percent of the total population.[6]

The older members appear to be more committed to tithing, or at least to regular giving, than our younger members. Persons who are long-time church members tend to increase their support over the years. These loyal members are contributing generously, but their years of service are not unlimited, and they are not being replaced. In 1985 the number of United Methodists who died increased by almost one thousand over the preceding year. As large numbers pass from the scene, the drop in income will be drastic.

It has become a practice for United Methodist leaders, when the membership statistics are released, to lament the annual decline in members, but to say, "Thank God the level of giving has held up and even increased somewhat." It is true that giving by United Methodists has continued to increase. Between 1970 and 1983 Methodism increased its expenditures for all purposes by 183 percent.[7] This is the money spent by all churches for local expenses (salaries, program, building expenses, and so on) and contributed to the denomination for administration, missions, and other benevolent causes.

However, the 1970s was a period of high inflation. To get an accurate picture of the financial trends, it is necessary to hold inflation constant and consider the purchasing power of the dollar.[8] When this is done, one sees that an increase in the purchasing power of United Methodist expenditures grew not by 183 percent, but by only 11 percent. But this is a significant gain when it is compared to the membership decrease of 13 percent during the same period. To put it another way, 13 percent fewer church members contributed 11 percent more money in 1983 than in 1970. Persons who have been members for a long time tend to have a high degree of commitment, which is expressed in a high level of giving.

Two significant shifts in the allocation of funds within The United Methodist Church took place during this period. First, *benevolent and mission causes received a smaller share of the funds.* These causes received 16 percent of the total money in 1970; by 1983 this had dropped to 13 percent. The largest proportion of our benevolent and mission funds come from our larger churches—churches that have enough "surplus" funds left over after meeting their own internal needs to send to denominational projects.

During the past quarter of a century, a large number of our once large and vibrant urban congregations have either drastically declined or closed. A few examples will illustrate this tragic trend. In 1960 the Barton Heights Church (Richmond, Virginia) had 1,031 members, Narden Park (Detroit, Michigan) had 2,401, and City Church (Gary, Indiana) had 1,687. Today none of these congregations exists.

The list of the once large churches that have declined by more than half in the past twenty-five years includes: Wesley Monumental, Savannah, Georgia (54 percent); First, Evanston, Illinois (65 percent); First, Pittsburgh, Pennsylvania (56 percent); Elm Park, Scranton, Pennsylvania (69 percent); Trinity, Denver, Colorado (61 percent); First, Los Angeles, California (85 percent); McCoy, Birmingham, Alabama (85 percent); and Linwood Boulevard, Kansas City, Missouri (91 percent). The loss and drastic decline of these congregations

19

signals not only a tragic loss of ministry to these urban areas, but also a potential dramatic decline in funds available for our church-wide and mission programs. In 1985, the 4 percent of United Methodist congregations of one thousand or more members provided 25 percent of the World Service Funds and Conference Benevolences.[9]

The losses in the once large urban churches have not been replaced by new congregations in the suburbs. During the nine years from 1950 to 1958, The Methodist church organized 1,053 new churches.[10] In the fourteen year period from 1970 to 1984, only 597 new churches were started.[11] To put it another way, between 1950 and 1958 we started an average of 117 churches each year; between 1970 and 1984 we started an average of 43 churches each year.

Second, *a greater share of the mission and benevolent contributions is being retained by the regional judicatories.* In 1970, the national church agencies received 39 percent of the benevolent income; by 1983 this proportion had dropped to 33 percent. The remaining money was retained for use in the region by the annual conferences. These data indicate that in a period of financial stringency the needs closest to home will be met first. The local congregation will receive priority over the denomination. The regional judicatory will be funded ahead of the national and world denomination. It's not that we have become more selfish or locally concerned, but that we have less money left over after meeting local maintenance needs.

This is further illustrated by an examination of United Methodist expenditures for missions and other benevolences for the period from 1970 to 1983, while holding inflation constant. The purchasing power of the funds provided to the national church actually declined by 26 percent. The purchasing power of the funds provided to the regional judicatories also decreased, but only by 4 percent. It is ironic that, in a period in which United Methodists were congratulating themselves on becoming more globally concerned, our actual financial commitment to global ministry dramatically declined.

Toward Revitalization

Despite the significance of the decrease in membership for the immediate and the long-term future of The United Methodist Church, the drop in membership is primarily a symptom of deeper problems. The membership decline will not be reversed only by addressing it per se by attempting to recruit new people. Working harder at what we have been doing will not get to the causes of the problem. When we don't know what to do, we urge greater sincerity and effort in doing what we have always done—such as the 1984 General Conference call to more than double the membership to twenty million by 1992. Frustration will be the inevitable result. Such activity may bring in a few more people, but it will not address the United Methodist malaise. It will, at best, provide temporary relief, like taking an aspirin but failing to deal with the real cause of the pain. At worst, temporary, superficial modifications will produce greater disillusionment and synicism when they don't work.

We are convinced that United Methodists must give their attention to the specific issues that are causing the membership decrease. This means looking beyond the symptoms to the roots of the problem. The goal of the church is not, of course, to gain numbers for the sake of the numbers. It is to be faithful to the gospel and to win people to Jesus Christ. The statistical trends are not an end in themselves but one way to measure whether what the church is doing is effective. Those who dismiss the measurement of mission by reference to financial and demographic statistics as merely "playing the numbers game" are evading the clear truth that numbers mean people and commitment. Our church was born through Wesley's creative and courageous response to institutional malaise in his own established Anglican Church. What a church does or does not do at a particular time may increase or decrease its effectiveness. In the pages that follow, we shall present some specific proposals concerning what The United Methodist Church can do to be revitalized and to increase the effectiveness of its witness.

Our study is based on five assumptions. First, we are convinced that a revitalized church is not only possible, but it is also what United Methodism ought to be. Our goal is not a larger institution but a church that is vital, effective, and faithful in carrying out its mission.

Second, Christian people, including leaders of the church, have the freedom to decide how they will respond to the demands of the gospel not only in their personal lives, but also in their collective life. They decide what the church as an institution shall and shall not do. Their actions have consequences that are either positive or negative. To us has been entrusted the power to communicate the gospel. We don't create salvation—God has already done that in Jesus Christ. But we, like every church before us, can either hide our light under a bushel of organizational inadequacy, or we can let it shine before all people. The major responsibility rests on us.

Third, the way in which the church carries on its work will vary, depending to a great degree on the socio-cultural context of a particular time and place. As the society changes, the church must change its method. The industrialization and urbanization of eighteenth-century England created new situations that the Wesleyan movement creatively addressed, which the Church of England, until Wesley, mostly ignored. In our own history, we have a warning about the peril of doing what we have always done. Institutions tend to continue carrying on once-successful programs long after they have become outmoded and useless. Christian churches are not exempt from this phenomenon. What we have been doing is not producing the results we want today.

Fourth, revitalization tends not to come from those who hold positions of authority and power in an institution. Our leaders, particularly those in our vast bureaucracy, may not be those best able to lead if leadership involves basic, perhaps painful, change. Such persons may use the rhetoric of reform, for most of them like to think of themselves as social activists. An occasional prophetic voice is heard crying in the wilderness of denominational structure. However, in the final analysis most persons in the institutional hierarchy and bureaucracy will find genuine reform too threatening to their present positions and find ways to oppose it either openly or subtly. Change requires redistribution of power, and those who have power want to preserve it. Revitalization will inevitably produce conflict. We know that, in preaching the need for change in our church, we bring not the peace of the *status quo,* but the sword of innovation.

Fifth, the entire denomination cannot be revitalized by official actions and churchwide programs. We need no new "missional priority" for what we propose here. Revitalization can come only if enough lay members who have no vested interest in the denominational hierarchy and bureaucracy and enough ministers who are willing to risk their minimal vested interest take the necessary bold actions. We already have the structure and the means to change what needs to be changed. In the pages that follow, we shall describe what actions need to be taken for United Methodism to move into its third century as a vital and more effective church.

Notes

1. This group formed the Evangelical Church of North America in Portland, Oregon, which now has 127 congregations and over 11,500 members.

2. Methodist statistics are from the annual editions of the *General Minutes of the Annual Conferences of The United Methodist Church* (Council on Finance and Administration, Evanston, Ill., 1968–1985). Rates of change have been computed by the authors.

3. Data provided by the Section on Records and Statistics, General Council on Finance and Administration, Evanston, Illinois.

4. *The Episcopal Church Annual* (Wilson, Conn.: Morehouse Barlow Company, 1985), p. 19.

5. The figures for the denominations, except United Methodist and Episcopal, are from Constant H. Jacquet, Jr., ed. *Yearbook of American Churches* (New York: Council Press, 1970) and Constant H. Jacquet, Jr., ed., *Yearbook of American and Canadian Churches* (Nashville: Abingdon Press, 1985). Rates of change have been computed by the authors.

6. "The Case of the Missing Numbers," *Discipleship Trends,* vol. IV, no. 4, August, 1986 (General Board of Discipleship, The United Methodist Church).

7. The financial data for The United Methodist Church are from the *Annual Report of the General Council on Finance and Administration of the United Methodist Church* (Evanston, Ill., 1970 and 1984).

8. To control for inflation, the Consumer Price Index was used to convert the funds into 1967 dollars.

9. Data provided by the Section on Records and Statistics, General Council on Finance and Administration, Evanston, Illinois.

10. Roy A. Sturm, *Methodism's New Churches 1950–1958* (Philadelphia; Department of Research and Survey, Division of National Missions, Board of Missions of The Methodist Church, 1958), p. 1.

11. Douglas W. Johnson, *A Study of New Churches 1966–1984* (New York: National Program Division, General Board of Global Ministries, 1986), p. 2.

Recover the Real Purpose of the Church

Chapter 2. He spoke out of his personal frustration, but his outburst reflected the sentiments of many other laypersons on the Council on Ministries at that night's meeting. "Food closets, yoga classes, youth trips to Disney World, resolutions on Central America—would somebody please tell me the business of this church?"

After a time of awkward silence, another person said, "If my company did business like the church, we wouldn't be in business for long. What is our product? Who are our customers? What do we offer that no one else is selling?"

Of course, the church is not a business. Jesus Christ is not a product, and those who are unchurched are not merely potential customers, but these frustrated laypersons do have a most valid question. *What is the purpose of the church?*

Uncertain Purpose

Across United Methodism, there are scores of congregations and their pastors who have become debilitated because of unfocused, unrealistic, unbiblical understandings—or should we say, biblical misunderstandings—about the nature and purpose of the Christian church. The early goal of the Methodists and EUBs to "spread scriptural holiness throughout the land" has become a diffused, poorly defined mandate to be all things to all people. Who are we and what are we supposed to be doing as United Methodists?

One response might be that we are supposed to be everywhere doing everything. "The world is my parish"—Wesley's retort when he was expelled from Anglican pulpits—has been taken as a mandate by latter-day United Methodists to be involved everywhere, attempting to meet every human need. Besides, Christianity is an incarnational faith: "God so loved the world." Our involvement in the world, our pronouncements, programs, resolutions, and breathless activity is our United Methodist way of testifying to the reality of the Incarnation. God loved the world, God came into the world in the Christ, so we also ought to be in the world.

But why in the world and to what purpose? The gospel is not simply a generalized call to be in the world, but a call to be there *in the name of Christ.* The gospel, rather than the needs of the world, defines the mission of the church. In fact, apart from the gospel, the world does not know what it needs. Many in the world may feel that they need an organization that confirms their innate human values, fulfills their selfish desires, and helps them to be ever more self-centered. The Incarnation does not mean that every human desire is a valid human need, that the church exists to give the youth somewhere fun to go on Friday nights. Many socially desirable activities cannot and should not be the responsibility of the church. The Incarnation is about the invasion into human history of God in the form of Jesus of Nazareth, who came calling people to be his disciples in a new kingdom.

Throughout the centuries, later disciples of Jesus have had to define and redefine themselves carefully. Every reformation of the church has been, in great part, a debate about the purpose of the church. Wesley's own revival was born out of his argument with the eighteenth-century Church of England over its failure to attend to the demands of the gospel for change of heart and life and its unwillingness to reach out to the masses of people. Reformations and revivals, like those led by Wesley, seem necessary for the rejuvenation of the church, perhaps because the church is constantly tempted to forsake its God-given mission in favor of a more socially acceptable and comfortable function. Since religion deals with every aspect of human life, it is all too easy for the church to become lost in harried attention to this and that, breathlessly attempting to catch the next wind of cultural change, rather than to keep its sights on the specific things the Christian faith wants to do for human life.

A denomination that lacks a consensus about the theological purpose of the church becomes compulsive in its efforts to be busy in much activity. It dares not stop to ask itself about the value of its activities, because it has lost confidence that it has the answer. Blown to and fro by each passing fad, this chuch eventually gives the impression that it is like the Pecos River—six inches deep and a mile wide.

A Misguided Self-Perception

For a number of generations, The United Methodist Church was able to think of itself as a sort of national church, the nearest thing to a state church that existed in America. We were the largest, most representative, and (so we assumed) the most influential of all American Protestant bodies. It was, therefore, our duty to help run the country, to be a church that, like the medieval Roman Catholic Church before us, sought to permeate every area of life with our influence. It was our duty to speak out on every social issue because, in a sense, this was "our" country. We enjoyed thinking of ourselves as a major force in the society, an organization with political clout. Traditional Wesleyan social concern had become political activism—drafting resolutions to Congress, lobbying for "our" side of some issue, pressuring legislators to vote "our" way, forming caucus groups, and becoming part of coalitions with other church and secular organizations.

Much of this political activism in the name of The United Methodist Church was based on at least two erroneous assumptions about the purpose of the church. First, it assumed that the primary function of the church was to help run the United States. Our political activism was at worst an extension of our imperialistic assumption that this was "our" country and that we represented the consensus of what was best for all Americans. At best it was our attempt to be both powerful and responsible. Looking at our political assumptions from the vantage point of the late 1980s, we see that they seem anachronistic. We are gradually getting pushed out of the driver's seat in American society. If we ever had a claim to be America's national church, that claim is less credible now than at any time in this century. Our resolutions to Congress and to the President seem either arrogant or silly in the new climate. Who is listening to us?

Second, our political activism of the last few decades has made an erroneous assumption about the historic Wesleyan concern for the wider society. Early American Methodists and EUBs founded some of this country's earliest schools, colleges, homes for children, and hospitals. These institutions were founded, not to do something socially worthwhile for American society as a whole, but *to preserve the integrity of the church* within a society that, while seeming to be generally congenial to the goals of the Methodist movement, was a decidedly mixed blessing. The best way to serve this new country was to build a vibrant, self-conscious, clearly defined church. Methodism founded institutions to strengthen the church. Today we have inherited responsibility for institutions whose relationship to the church is at best tenuous, at worst nonexistent, other than their financial dependency.

Of course, if American society as a whole is judged to be roughly contiguous with The United Methodist Church, then there is no real need to worry about the integrity of the church. Being American is equal to being Christian. How can that claim be sustained? We are no longer a powerful, socially dominant institution that is able to speak with one voice to American society. We are a church that, in its tireless efforts to lean over to speak to American society, may have fallen over, engulfed by the predominant values of our society. Our church's colleges do not appear to be decidedly different from their secular counterparts. Our mission has been reduced to politics, our Social Principles mirror, to a great extent, to political opinions from one part (generally the left) of the secular political spectrum. When our church speaks, it speaks mostly in political terms rather than religious ones. The programs of many of our local chuches appear to be a mix of activities from the Y. M. C. A., the Garden Club, and the League of Women Voters. When our boards and agencies take it upon themselves to speak for and to direct United Methodists, divisiveness is created not only because many United Methodists disagree with the opinions of these boards and agencies, but also because many of the laity believe that these opinions are more influenced by secular ideology than Christian theology. Our internal squabbles over which political stand is most Christian resemble the factionalism of a national political party.

The United Methodist Church has fused and thereby confused its peculiarly Christian values with the dominant values of American culture. Consequently, it tends to align itself (on both the left and the right) with political policies. Because of this, there is a two-fold danger: either the confusion of religious and secular values is uncritically accepted, or an attempt is made to separate religious from secular values by those who fear the secular politization of the church. The church becomes either the mascot of society or a cowering escape from society.

The church has integrity; it has its own worship and mission, which is expressed through its life in society. The relation of the church to society is one in which the worship of God sends one out in service. Both sides are needed; each complements the other. The uniqueness of the church is in its worship, worship that is not a time of the week, but a way of life. In worship, we hold fast to Christ; to everything else we can hold loosely. No other policy, value, or person may challenge Christ's preeminence. By holding fast to Christ, we are freed to pursue the moral implications of service in Christ's name.

We are in the world as Christians. This means that we may take political stands; but they must be amenable to our prior commitment to Christ. We contend for justice, but justice that is continually reinterpreted by our commitment to Christ. We may challenge our, or any other, nation in so far as loyalty to Christ commands. Commitment to Christ and the world are both present, but the order and the level of commitment are important to maintain.

A Need for Boundaries

The United Methodist Church must recover a sense of its own integrity as a distinct phenomenon in American society. Integrity implies boundaries, limits, a discernible identity and focus of activity. The church is more than a society to provide social activities for its members, more than a platform for political agitation. The task of the church is much the same as the task Wesley gave to his societies: *to form a community of faith and practice that responds, in its life together and witness to the world, to the presence of Jesus Christ.* Formation of a visible people of God is the radical imperative preceding everything else the church is about. In a sense, the first "business" of the church is to be the church.

To some ears, this may sound introspective and isolationist. But the issue is not the simplistic alternative of whether the church will be "in the world," or whether we shall "serve the needs of the world." The questions are How? and For what ends? Christians are people who have been converted into a particular community with a particular world view, which recognizes Jesus Christ as Lord. This world view is generated by the stories, values, insights, and rituals that are reenacted and celebrated within the worship of the church. Because we know a story about one who was born in a stable, preached good news to the poor and the captives, healed the sick, was persecuted by the authorities, was crucified, and was raised, we find that we may have some peculiar notions of right and wrong, of just and unjust. In other words, our Christian political and social attitudes arise from the peculiar story that is the gospel of Jesus Christ. Our political task is not to be conservative, liberal, practical, or even American. Our task is to be faithful to the gospel as a church.

Perhaps one reason the world has difficulty in taking our social pronouncements seriously is that we have reduced our historic Wesleyan social concern to public posturing and slogans, pronouncements and resolutions, rather than the tougher task of building faithful, visible congregations that embody, in our life together, our dominant convictions. Rather than simply developing slogans about justice, we are to define Christian justice by our care of one another in the church. Rather than pleading with Congress to do right, we are to build a people of righteousness in our local congregations. This is how the church serves the world and affects the wider society—by being the church.

The Business of the Church

The church is the business of the church, not only because it is the place in which we learn Christian points of view, but it is also the place in which our point of view is embodied. The church's most signifcant political act is not some resolution we send to Congress or our participation in some boycott, but it is in being the church. Wesley believed that the church could be an alternative community, a visible, concrete, counter-cultural protest against the dominant social structures of the wider society. In their class meetings and societies, early Methodists pioneered new social structures based not on power or on abstract definitions of justice or on social or economic status, but on their members' common commitment to Christ and to his kingdom. Early Methodists indicted the established political order and challenged the social *status quo* by example rather than through resolutions and pronouncements.

The church is always judged by the sort of people it produces. If we cannot achieve justice and peace in the church, then there is no wonder that the rest of the world fails to take us seriously when we pontificate on some national concern. Why should the rest of American society listen to our bishops when they speak on nuclear war, unless the world can see that we have first, in The United Methodist Church, created those structures and relationships that make us a people of peace, a people who are willing to suffer for the cause of truth? Do we accept money that is earned from investment and work in defense industries? What specific, supportive guidance might we give United Methodists who work for and are economically dependent on the vast complex of military-related industries? Resolutions are cheap. Institutional embodiment is costly. We must again be a people whose political opinions are backed up by something more than self-congratulatory posturing. Unfortunately, rather than risk self-sacrifice or engage in mutual discipline of one another (the historic vision of Wesley), we have chosen to make pronouncements.

The church is a global, multi-national organization. The most important thing that we can do about the evil of South African Apartheid is not to offer advice to Congress about the specifics of governmental policy toward South Africa; Congress has shown little inclination to listen to United Methodists and little ability to understand why we hold our values. We already have a strong link with the Methodists who live and struggle in South Africa. Let us be supportive and in communication with those churches. Our church can be expected to have certain definite opinions about U.S.— Soviet relations because of the knowledge that we have many fellow Methodists in the Soviet Union. Our communication with them and our care for them in their struggles are more important to us even than the demands of the United States Department of State. The church's most effective political solution is the church—an alternative community that, by the quality of its own life, demonstrates that God, not nations, rules the world.

The church has the sometimes unpleasant task of noting that even those who are blessed with peace, freedom, and justice are sinners in need of God's grace—people whose time on earth is terminal; people whose innate fear, self-delusion, and insecurity often make them pervert even such noble words as peace, freedom, and justice. Therefore, the church will have a somewhat more expansive notion of what people need beyond the limits of politics.

When we lack a clear notion of what we are supposed to be doing as a church, we attempt to do everything. We succeed at little and appear to fail at everything. Our social concern becomes a shopping list of current causes, without thought to what the church does best.

The Pastor's Responsibility

"We asked our pastor to teach a church-wide Bible study," one layperson told us. "But he said that he was too busy. If he would let somene else manage the church gymnasium, and if he were not so consumed by his duties on the local school board, then he might have more time to be a pastor."

A generation ago, pastors were expected to preach, to teach, to visit the sick in the congregation, and to evangelize unchurched persons. Today our pastors seem unsure of what their job is, despite (or because of) the current *Discipline's* listing of twenty-one pastoral responsibilities.[1] Persons who were once called to preach the gospel and to guide the church have become exhausted by the drudgery of managing a large volunteer organization with a round of diverse activities. Or the pastor becomes the resident political activist and free-lance community worker, serving on community boards and fighting political battles, jobs that are better done by the laity rather than the pastor. The pastor is ordained to empower the laity for ministry. He or she is to minister to the ministers, and is not the one whose frenetic clerical activism becomes a substitute for lay activism. The less clearly defined are the pastor's specific functions, the more pastors take over the roles of the laity, thus driving the laity out of their baptismally bestowed duties for ministry.[2]

Lyle Schaller has observed that after a couple of decades of much rhetoric about the need for The United Methodist Church to "serve the community," most of our churches need to expend more effort and attention in helping the church to *be* a community. It is much more difficult to form a faithful congregation, even in these democratic United States (perhaps especially in these United States), than to do good works for the entire town.

Every United Methodist congregation would do well to spend time composing a "Statement of Purpose" for itself. This would be a purpose that the local people would own, not simply a statement handed down from a distant agency. All programs, budget items, leadership, and parish activities should then be judged on the basis of this statement of purpose. Our mandate is to "go therefore and make disciples of all nations, baptizing them in the name of the Father and of the Son and of the Holy Spirit" (Matt. 28:19). This is what the people called United Methodist must do.

Notes

1. *The Book of Discipline of the United Methodist Church 1984* (Nashville: The United Methodist Publishing House, 1984), par. 439, 440, 441.

2. In a book that pleads for the revitalization of lay ministry, it is noted that the attempt to address global needs has diverted us from addressing people's needs: "The liberal religious establishment . . . has abandoned the family to the therapeutic. It steadfastly ignores the moral, ethical, and lifestyle dilemmas of everyday living. It pursues a political and social agenda of issues so global and complex that most citizens despair of either comprehension or solution. Ordinary members, clergy or lay, are left to their own devices in addressing the stuff out of which they must spin the web of daily life." James D. Anderson and Ezra Earl Jones, *Ministry of the Laity* (San Francisco: Harper & Row, 1986), p. 21.

Affirm the Wesleyan Heritage

Chapter 3. Christian people have always organized themselves into self-conscious groups within the larger body of the church. There has been no time in the history of the church, from the earliest period to the present, when there have not been identifiable parties, followers of certain teachers, and adherents of particular doctrines. For the past five centuries, independent denominations have been the way that Western Christendom has been constituted. In the United States there are 212 Christian denominations that have provided statistics to the National Council of Churches.[1] This number has declined only slightly in the past twenty-five years despite mergers and realignments. A number of denominations do not provide data, so the figure 212 is a partial count. While the various Christian churches share a common origin and most beliefs, denominations based on both theological and sociological differences will continue to be with us.

Denominations are useful organizations. They provide the vehicle for witness and ministry. They allow for social and cultural diversity among God's people, so that such diversity is not a barrier to accepting the Christian faith. The individual can, therefore, find a local church within a particular denomination in which the language and the culture are familiar. The fact that denominations persist is an indication of their usefulness. A vital church is one that affirms its denominational heritage.

Why Our Heritage Has Been Downplayed

There has been much negative sentiment toward denominationalism, particularly in the second half of this century. Many have accepted the notion that denominations represent a surrender to human sinfulness; eventually this sin of separateness would be overcome and all of the churches would merge into one. While this would be an evolutionary process, its inevitability was accepted by many. Interdenominational cooperation would eventually give way to organizational or organic union.

The ecumenical movement has been viewed as the way the churches would ultimately be organizationally united. It should be noted, however, that the birth of the ecumenical movement coincided with the development of big business in America. The giant corporation was seen by church leaders as an example to be emulated. The consolidation of business was made a model for the churches. Josiah Strong, a leader of the Evangelical Alliance, took a practical, rather than a theological, approach to church union. In his book, *The New Era or the Coming Kingdom,* Strong states, "Business, open-eyed, has seen and seized the immense advantage which lies in consolidation, organization; but the Protestant churches do not yet appreciate this advantage."[2] The corporate model is still favored by many church leaders, although they tend not to be as explicit about their models as were their predecessors. Even though today's society challenges the dominance of the corporate giant (witness the breakup of the Bell telephone system), some church leaders still strive to create a religious monopoly. The creation of negative attitudes and feelings of guilt about denominations has contributed to their decline. Is it really true that our denomination is a hindrance to the gospel? Or is the particular heritage and structure of United Methodism a unique vehicle for the gospel?

Know Our History

A vital denomination must understand its past in order to minister to its present. Methodism began in eighteenth-century England, a difficult time and place for Christian belief and Christian life. The intellectual life of England was dominated by various Enlightenment influences. Many intellectuals equated religion with superstition, an outmoded vestige that thinking modern people would soon outgrow. Deism was all the rage within the universitites and among many Church of England clergy. Deism's limitation of faith to reason undercut Christian authority and proclamation. Newly discovered science was said to be the master of the future. The rational, autonomous individual became the self-assured center of intellectual and moral reality. Most people were more interested in nature than in revelation.

Coupled with this intellectual climate was widespread social deterioration, brought about by changes from a rural to an industrial society in England. Poor workers, uprooted from the security and the values of the farm, crowded into squalid cities and bleak factory towns. Alcoholism was a major social evil. Some of the rich profited from child labor in the mines, the lucrative African slave trade with the American colonies, and horrible conditions in the factories.

This was the world of John Wesley (1703–1791), *a world much like our own.* Whereas many of us have accepted our world as a given, a fact to be assimilated and accepted, an irresistible source of institutional decline, our spiritual forebears saw their world as something to be confronted, converted, and challenged with the love of God in Christ. Not content to see their beloved Church of England decline into a modest, backseat, vaguely civilizing influence on English cuture; not willing to accept the social evil around them as unalterably given, they trusted the power of the gospel to turn their world upside down. We must follow their example. By reclaiming where we have been as followers of Wesley, we can recover new direction and energy for the future.

Affirm Our Heritage

Great movements are dependent on great leaders (see chapter 5), and the Methodist Revival was no exception. The brothers, John and Charles Wesley, were reared within a Church of England rectory by strong parents. John was a natural leader with strong commitments. While a student at Oxford, he became the leader of a group of devout students who followed rigorous spiritual disciplines in order to strengthen themselves as Christians. The characteristics of this little group—exact discipline, sacramental rigors, visitation of prisons, study and prayer, mutual encouragement and correction—became life-long, distinctive characteristics of Wesley's approach to Christian formation. The group was derided by scoffing fellow students, who called them the Holy Club, Bible Moths, and Methodists.

After Oxford, the Wesleys had an unsuccessful stint as missionaries in Georgia. Their work was ineffective, principally because of their rigidity and inability to work with the rough colonists and Native Americans. On shipboard, returning to England, John encountered a group of Moravians who told him of their conviction of the need for an assured, inner experience of Jesus Christ as Savior, an experience the Wesleys had not had. Their spirits were troubled until May of 1738. First Charles and then John underwent moving conversion experiences. John wrote in his *Journal:* "I felt my heart strangely warmed. I felt I did trust in Christ, Christ alone for salvation; and an assurance was given me that He had taken away *my* sin, even *mine,* and saved *me* from the law of sin and death." The event compelled Wesley to undertake his ministry afresh, risking, experimenting, organizing to "spread scriptural holiness over the land."

Wesley was a demanding, compulsive, and autocratic (by our standards) leader who subjugated everything to the new movement and expected his followers to do likewise. With immense energy, he set out to do nothing less than to evangelize his whole nation. In a straightforward, direct style, Wesley preached to the underclass around the mining pits, on the depressed edges of the cities, and in the open fields.

Although he had received the best Oxford education, Wesley refused to carry on theology in the academic style. Theology, for him, was the servant of the church. He did not trouble himself about theological systems or expend energy on speculation about the existence of God or whether the divine could be made credible to modern people. He started with his own experience of the grace of God, an experience that was more real to Wesley and to the "people called Methodists" than any abstract speculation. Rational argument always took a back seat to the experience of the presence of God and to the proclamation of God's grace.

John Wesley felt a strong mandate to reach the mass of people who were unchurched and had not responded to the gospel. The first time he tried field preaching, he used as his text, "The Spirit of the Lord is upon me, because he hath anointed me to preach the gospel to the poor." For the most part, he did not seek out or attempt to evangelize the upper classes. No Methodist preaching post was established in any of the five most privileged boroughs of London.

The poor heard him gladly. In his preaching and writing, Wesley returned to the source: the Bible. He intended to be a biblical theologian. Although he stressed the need for all belief and practice to be tested by experience, reason, and church tradition, scripture was the fundamental source for theology and the ultimate court of appeal in differences of opinion. The two principal resources that Wesley left to guide his followers are his *Sermons* and his *Notes on the New Testament.*

His preaching centered on the grace of God. Although he never lapsed into fuzzy thinking or mushy affirmations of theological vagaries, such as "pluralism," Wesley was determined to stress the central truths of faith and to leave divisive arguments about minor "opinions" to others. For Wesley, theology served the interest of Christian formation; "practical divinity" is what interested him. Theology was not an end in itself, but the means for transformed "holy living and dying." We are born sinners, even those whose most sincere and earnest actions are flawed. Unlike more optimistic assessors of human nature, Wesley was able to be so honest about human sin because he was so confident of the love of God toward sinners. Salvation is the free gift of God's grace apart from our good works, perhaps even in spite of our good works.

Then of what value is holy living? The tension between faith and works was the theological problem that Wesley confronted. Regeneration and new birth are given by God, but the resulting new life is expressed in love of God and neighbor. Wesley discovered that the Reformation emphasis on "faith alone" apart from "holy living" often undercut the Christian's moral life. The two must be held together. As United Methodist theologian Albert Outler has said, Wesley

> evangelized the Christian ethic and moralized the Christian evangel, . . . that repudiated both human self-assertion and passivity. He turned out "rules" by the dozen—but also with warnings that even the most scrupulous rule-keeping will get you only to the state of being an "almost Christian."[3]

While stressing that we are indeed sinners, that God's love in Christ is our only path to redemption and happiness, Wesley also stressed "Christian perfection," perhaps his most controversial assertion. "Christians are called to *love God with all their heart and to serve Him with all their strength:* which is precisely what I apprehended to be meant by the scriptural term perfection," said Wesley.[4] The stress on perfection was congruent with Wesley's intention to link faith and works, salvation and ethics. Christians are those who constantly examine every area of their lives and order each affection, each desire, and each act in accordance with divine will. In stressing sanctification—Christian formation—Wesley wedded the Protestant stress on justification with the Roman Catholic stress on holy living. Instantaneous new birth is followed by a lifelong process of sanctification. John Wesley asserted the value of regular participation in the corporate worship of the church through prayer, Bible reading, fasting, Christian conference, and the Lord's Supper. This is in contrast to some Protestants of his day (and our own), because these "ordinary means of grace," as Wesley called the sacraments and the church, strengthen and perfect us. The Wesleyan stress on Christian formation, education, attack on social evils and destructive personal habits, the duty of constant communion, and the necessity for membership within a supportive group of fellow Christians can all be attributed to his emphasis on perfection.

If Wesley had only been a great preacher or a popular writer, we would have had no United Methodist Church. He organized his followers because he knew that no one can sustain the Christian life alone—the Christian faith must be institutionally embodied through creative political, social, and structural arrangements that enable us to be transformed into the new creations that God intends for us to be. Wesley formed his people into "societies," large groups that assembled for preaching and spiritual instruction, and "classes," small, disciplined groups of about twelve persons who gathered for prayer, mutual support, and study. Even smaller "bands" of four or five persons met for closer spiritual direction. The formation of these small groups was the organizational stroke of genius of Methodism. Not content simply to gain enthusiastic converts who could point to some vague emotional experience as the source of their discipleship, Wesley organized people into a structure whereby they received the support, correction, and encouragement they needed to live as Christians in a society that operated from a set of assumptions other than the gospel. Confident that they had experienced a reality greater than that of the world, these Methodists sought to embody and to inculcate the Spirit of Christ, to make people who, in their daily living, resembled Christ. Wesley knew enough about human nature and the nature of the gospel to know that no individual alone can sustain this hope, can embody the Christian life-style. Therefore, he created structures of corporate life, which enabled the Methodists to produce the sort of disciples they believed the gospel deserved. In salvation, God takes the initiative in reaching out to us in Jesus Christ. But we must respond through a concrete, communal embodiment of our response to God's initiative. Wesley, as well as Asbury, Otterbein, and Albright, really believed that Christians are "called to be saints," called to "perfection"—that is, maturity of thought and faithfulness of life-style. In other words, Wesley was convinced that the church is in the business of producing Christian character.

Recovering Our Heritage

Some time between then and now, we succumbed to the notion that the church is in the business of character affirming rather than character producing. Somehow we bought the idea that the task of the Christan life is adjustment to what is, rather than conversion and sanctification into what ought to be. Lacking confidence in our ability to specify the exact shape of Christian character, we ceased trying to form distinctively Christian life-styles. One of our current sources of membership loss is our inability to retain our young people, after their maturity, in our church. When they become adults, too many of our children leave The United Methodist Church for other denominations, while others drop out of the church altogether. Decades of haphazard Christian education, the ethics of cultural accommodation, non-biblical preaching, and neglect of the task of formation have left us with a bitter harvest. Our theology succumbed to the same individualism, feel-good-do-your-own-thing morality, and narcissistic attitudes as the rest of American society. You don't need a church when there is little distinction between the Christian way and the American way.

Yet there is reason to be optimistic about future possibilities for our church because the Wesleyan heritage, if we recover it in our church life and thought, makes United Methodists uniquely suited to the challenges of our time. Increasing numbers of people long for meaning in life, meaning beyond their own selfish interests, meaning not of their sole creation, meaning that gives their lives significance by joining them to some project greater than themselves. Millions of our fellow Americans have not heard the gospel or seen it enacted in such a way as to call forth their commitment. Millions more have earnestly tried to live the Christian life on their own, but have become frustrated and defeated because they have sought to be Christians in a way that Wesley knew was impossible—on their own, without a supportive, connected, disciplined community of fellow believers.

Here are the unique aspects of our heritage, which are our legitimate birthright as the heirs of Wesley and which need to be reasserted and reclaimed in our day:

1. *The experience of the grace of God is the central fact of the gospel.* Wesley affirmed "think and let think" in matters of tangential and extraneous Christian opinions. He did so, not because he affirmed "pluralism" (a polite, contemporary way of saying that we are hopelessly fragmented in our beliefs) or because he thought that theology doesn't make any difference.[5] He was determined to keep his followers focused on the central, irreducible, non-negotiable theological affirmation of the Christian faith. Christians are those who have all their thoughts, affections, actions, and efforts transformed by personal experience of the grace of God. Our church has become distracted in a variety of competing and contradictory theologies of this and that and have raised a number of extraneous "opinions" to the level of doctrine. In his evangelistic efforts, Wesley never tried to be all things to all people or to accommodate the Christian witness to the intellectual fads of his day. In fact, his revival was an assertive challenge to the most widely accepted and enthusiastically held social and intellectual values of the eighteenth century. United Methodists must take a cue from Wesley and reassert the biblical bedrock of belief.

2. *Christian formation is the central purpose of the church and the goal of the Christian life.* Wesley indicated that God's design in raising up these preachers called Methodist was to reform the nation, more specifically, the church, and to spread scriptural holiness throughout the land. For us, the Christian faith is more than a noble philosophy of life, more than a warm, individual emotional experience. The Christian faith has to do with the making of holy people who are so formed by the love of Christ that they know the cost of discipleship and are willing to pay. Failing at formation, we either try to make the Christian faith credible to every thinking, sensitive

American, or we make generalized political pronouncements to the society as a whole. The recent bishops' statement on nuclear arms, for instance, calls for discusssion and debate among United Methodists and for action by Congress. But it never speaks directly to how contemporary United Methodists might risk forming our lives in such a way that we become witnesses for peace. Holy living and dying require self-discipline, cost, risk, and sacrifice; perhaps that is why we have forsaken the Wesleyan call to perfection in favor of pronouncements. Yet, our people are as hungry for order, adventure, and meaning in their lives as were the Bristol coal miners who heard Wesley.

3. *The gospel demands to be preached and lived before all.* Contemporary United Methodists know enough of the story of our origins to be shocked that our church has basically abandoned the task of evangelizing our society and has settled down to keep house within our own churches. We have switched from an evangelization-mission mode of operation to a maintenance mode. Some of our leaders have accepted the decline in membership as an unhappy fact of life, blaming it on irresistible forces of secularization. Rather than to evangelize the rapidly exploding ethnic minority populations in our country, we have decided to subsidize and to be content with the small proportion of ethnic churches we already have. We have trained our clergy so well that few of them seem able to lead in the evangelization of the poor and the oppressed, ill equipped as they are to preach the gospel and to form churches among those whom Oxford-educated Wesley saw as the chief recipients of the gospel. Wesley's fear that his "people called Methodist" would become wealthy and complacent, custodians of great buildings and guardians of the *status quo,* has become a reality. Yet, we have, in our heart of hearts, the memory of a church that once transformed English society and moved across America, not by intending to transform society, but by proclaiming God's gracious Word to all. We are, therefore, encouraged by recent calls to rekindle the fire of evangelism and growth. We believe that growth lies, as it did for Wesley, in the creative formation of new structures that turn our intentions into institutional realities.

The Wesleyan revival took hold and continued, even increased in momentum, after Wesley's death, in great part because Wesley channeled the spiritual energy that was ignited through his preaching into an effective, efficient, and functional organization that knew what it was doing and had the structure to do it. By taking seriously the perennial tasks of Christian formation, care, and accountability, Wesley bequeathed to us a heritage that gives us the means of revitalizing today's church.

Notes

1. Constant H. Jacquet, Jr., ed., *Yearbook of American and Canadian Churches* (Nashville: Abingdon Press, 1984), p. 244.

2. Josiah Strong, *The New Era or the Coming Kingdom* (New York: Baker & Taylor Co., 1893), p. 296.

3. Albert Outler, "The Place of Wesley in the Christian Tradition," in *The Place of John Wesley in the Christian Tradition*, ed. Kenneth E. Rowe (Metuchen, N. J.: Scarecrow Press, 1976), p. 22.

4. John Telford, ed., *The Letters of the Reverend John Wesley*, 8 vols. (London: Epworth Press, 1931), vol. 3, pp. 120-21.

5. Mark Horst, "The Problem of Theological Pluralism," *The Christian Century*, vol. 103, no. 33, November 5, 1986, pp. 971-74.

Serve the Church Instead of the Clergy

Chapter 4. A district superintendent in the West, after participating in a difficult cabinet meeting at which appointments had been discussed, commented, "Unless we make some changes, the preachers' union is going to wreck The United Methodist Church."

The clergy alone have not caused the membership decline or the malaise within the denomination. Nor will they alone be able to turn the church around. But, because of their critical role as leaders of both the congregations and the denomination, pastors must inevitably carry a large share of the responsibility for the current situation and can have a greater impact on reversing the trend than can the laity. Recent trends leading to increased clericalization of our church must be reversed if our clergy are to lead effectively.

The United Methodist System of Clergy Placement

The United Methodist Church has had a unique system of assigning clergy as compared to most of Protestantism. The pastor is appointed by a bishop who has the authority "to make and fix the appointments . . . " and "to divide or to unite circuit(s), station(s), or mission(s) as judged necessary for missional strategy and then to make appropriate appointments" (*Discipline,* par. 516.1 and 516.2). Pastors, by virtue of their election to conference membership and ordination, have entered into a covenant with all the ordained elders of the annual conference. The *Discipline* states that, "They offer themselves without reserve to be appointed and to serve, after consultation, as the appointive authority may determine" (par. 421). The United Methodist pastor has agreed to go where sent. The bishop is required to appoint every full member of the annual conference.

The clergy, not the lay members, determine who shall be admitted into the United Methodist ordained ministry. The only part that laypersons have in the process is at the very beginning, when the Pastor-Parish Relations Committee and the charge conference of the church of which the individual is a member recommend him or her to become a candidate for the ordained ministry. In the ensuing seven to ten years during the individual's candidacy, the decisions are made by members of the clergy only. The responsibility for deciding who shall become clergy is in the hands of those who are already clergy.

In the early days of the Methodist Episcopal Church in America, the clergy had some of the characteristics of a monastic order. They were assigned by the bishop to their circuits for periods of a year or less. They were expected to devote their entire energies to their work. Marriage, while not prohibited, was discouraged. The elder who married often found it necessary to "locate," that is, to withdraw from the itinerant ministry and become a local preacher.

Much of the world of the late twentieth century bears little resemblance to that of the early nineteenth. Nevertheless some of the values of the early circuit riders are as appropriate for today as they were almost two centuries ago. These include a willingness of the clergy to devote themselves entirely to the spreading of the gospel, giving their ministry priority over personal concerns, and being willing to go where the church feels they are most needed.

The United Methodist Church has had an effective system of admitting persons into the ordained ministry and placing them in local churches. It is a system that ensures that the ministers will have the freedom to preach the gospel. Because pastors are appointed by the bishop, they cannot be discharged by a majority vote of the congregation, as is the case in some denominations. Furthermore, every full member of an annual conference is guaranteed an appointment. This system allows the skills of a specific pastor to be matched with the needs of a congregation at a particular time. The appointive system permits women, minority, and younger and older clergy to be assigned to churches that might, under ordinary circumstances, not desire them. This results in the clergy, themselves, having the responsibility for ensuring that their peers maintain high standards of performance and conduct.

All of the above characteristics are positive and need to be continued. However any system is subject to abuse and can be used in ways that do not serve the best interests of the entire church. When a good system goes awry, it can be very difficult to change. People tend to remember the way it used to be and to emphasize the positive aspects. They may be reluctant to act because they don't know what to do or are afraid they will make a bad situation worse. Institutional inertia sets in.

The Seniority System

There has developed for the ministerial members of the annual conferences an informal, but clearly recognized and accepted, seniority system. It is not contained in the *Discipline* or any annual conference's standing rules, but it is adhered to with great care. United Methodist clergy are expected to follow a career track that begins in churches of small membership, often a circuit of two or more congregations located in a rural community. With the passage of time, a minister "pays his or her dues" in such appointments, but expects to "move up" to larger urban and more prestigious churches. There is, of course, nothing wrong with allowing young pastors to gain experience and rewarding those who have served effectively.

However, the problem with the United Methodist seniority system is twofold. First, it is extremely rigid. Generally, there is little likelihood of younger pastors' being appointed to large congregations until they are at least middle aged or even nearing the end of their careers. This is true even if a church desperately needs the energy and skills of a specific individual. The appointment often goes to a particular pastor, some "good soldier," as a reward for long and faithful (even if not too effective) service. It is rare to find an instance anywhere in the denomination in which the talented younger pastor, someone with less than twenty-five or thirty years in the ministry, is appointed to a large church. If professional baseball were run like The United Methodist Church, the Dwight Goodens would have to wait in the minor leagues until the Pete Roses had retired. One looks almost in vain across United Methodism for young pastors on the "fast track," persons being deliberately given the experience to be the denominational leaders of tomorrow.

Two actual examples will illustrate this problem. The first involves a pastor in his late thirties, who has served several appointments with distinction. His record includes growth in membership and an increase in support of mission projects in every church he has served. The district superintendent asked him to indicate the type of church that he would next like to serve. The pastor named an old, prestigious, but declining central city church and said he would like to see if he could turn it around. The superintendent laughingly responded, "It will be twenty years before you will get a chance at a church like that."

The second example involves a pastor who has just turned sixty. He has had a long and effective ministry and is currently serving a growing suburban congregation. In reflecting on his appointments, he said, "I don't think the church has used me well. Personally, I have no complaints, but I should have been assigned to a church like I have today about fifteen years ago. I think I could have given my best service then. I had the experience and the energy and certainly could have done more for the church in a community like this than where I was then serving."

The second aspect of the problem is the use of the pastor's salary as virtually the sole criterion to determine the individual's next appointment. The myth prevails that the higher the salary, the more effective the pastor. District superintendents urge churches to keep their salaries high so that they can be assured of having the best possible pastor appointed. Laypeople are led to believe that a high salary will assure that they will receive an effective pastor. This may or may not be true. Their next pastor may be a person of great dedication and ability or simply an individual who has achieved enough seniority to be appointed to a church that pays the amount the congregation offers.

A church that sets even a fairly high salary cannot be assured that a large number of pastors will be considered for the appointment. In point of fact, it is likely that only those clergy in the salary level just below the one being offered will be considered. One Pastor-Parish Relations Committee was told by the district superintendent that there were only thirteen ministers at the appropriate salary level (which was the step below the amount being offered). Only these could be considered for promotion to that chuch. The superintendent went on to say that seven or eight of these pastors were not in a position to move, so that actually only five or six pastors could be considered for the church. This shocked some of the laypersons on the committee. Because their church was one of the larger congregations in the annual conference, they assumed that the bishop would have a fairly large pool of ministers from which to select their next pastor.

The reason there is the greatest reluctance to tamper with the seniority system is the unwritten, but strictly followed, rule that no minister shall ever receive a reduction in salary. This, again, is a good practice, but because of the rigidness with which it is adhered to, it is one which also causes serious problems. A younger minister cannot be appointed to a church that pays a salary higher than he or she would be expected to receive at that point in his or her career because the next appointment would have to be at an even larger salary. To do so would put the seniority system out of balance.

The person who causes great consternation for the system is the younger pastor who, on her or his own, makes a large congregation out of a small one. In one case, a minister was appointed to a small urban congregation. In the course of a few years, he had recruited a large number of new members. This resulted in an equally large increase in the church's budget, including the amount contributed to the denominational benevolence programs and a corresponding increase in the minister's salary. However, the salary was not out of line for congregations of the size to which the membership had grown. This minister was the source of great concern to the judicatory officials. One district superintendent asked the key question, "Where can we send a man as young as he is at the salary that he is currently making?" Despite the fact that this pastor was effective at bringing people into the church and increasing the congregation's contributions to missions, he was perceived not as an asset but as an appointment problem. Too often, rigid adherence to the seniority system rewards mediocrity and punishes excellence.

The tragedy of the present seniority system is that it very often results in bad matches of ministers and congregations. When salary level and years of service become the most important factors (alas the *only* factors), ministers are sent to chuches in which the skills of the pastor are not appropriate to the needs of the congregation. The mission of the church receives less attention than the professional advancement of the minister. The pastor who is effective in a stable county seat town is sent to a growing suburban community. His personality, skills, and style of ministry are not appropriate for the church and community to which he has been sent. The result is that the church does not receive the leadership that is needed, and the pastor is frustrated because he knows that he is not being effective. Under the seniority system, the only option is to allow the pastor to remain for what would be considered the normal length of time and then to move him to a church with a slightly higher salary level. Over the long term, neither the clergy nor the congregations are well served by such a system.

When urged to disregard the seniority system, bishops and district superintendents often respond, "It would kill morale among our pastors." Is this true? The present system is killing the morale of the best clergy and the most deserving congregations. Clergy cynically speak of the present system as one in which ministers can "flop to the top," knowing that their appointment is a matter of salary and years of service rather than productivity. Congregations feel abused when they realize that someone was sent to them for no other reason than "she made $15,000 at her last appointment, and your church pays $15,500."

Every time a bishop or district superintendent tells a pastor, "Even though your gifts equip you to serve that church, I can't send you there yet because the salary is too high," or "You are going to that church because you are now making $15,000 and that church pays $15,500," they demoralize the most effective clergy and reinforce the notion of the least effective that it makes little difference what they do in a congregation—the system will keep them and promote them regardless of their work. The unwritten, unprescribed, and unlegislated clergy seniority system is demoralizing the church and its clergy.

Where Priority Is Placed

A decade ago Lyle E. Schaller wrote about what he called "the Big Revolution" taking place in American society. He stated, "For centuries people were trained to fit into the existing structures, patterns, schedules and traditions of the culture. . . . Increasingly the emphasis is to change the culture to accommodate people and to affirm the differences among people."[2] In the past decade, we have seen this trend continue until virtually every institution in society is under pressure to adjust to the perceived needs and desires of both individuals and groups.

This has some positive aspects. Institutions can become rigid and attempt to force persons into preconceived patterns that are neither good for the individual nor helpful to the institution. On the other hand, the purposes for which an institution was created can be thwarted if the institution is forced to adjust to a wide variety of individual desires.

Aspects of this "Big Revolution" can be found in The United Methodist Church, particularly among the clergy. Consider the amount of time and attention an annual conference gives to matters concerning the well being of the clergy and the ways that the clergy are attempting to make the church adjust to their particular needs and desires; items such as salary levels, pensions, travel, continuing education, parsonages, utilities, and various other clergy benefits occupy a prominent place on the agenda. These are, of course, relevant and important matters; pastors need to be fairly compensated.

What is increasingly evident is that the clergy are being influenced by the trend in the larger society and attempting to have the church adjust to their desires. The debate over whether the minister should live in a church-owned parsonage or purchase a home is an example. The debate has focused on whether owning a home is economically advantageous or emotionally satisfying to the pastor, not whether it contributes to or detracts from the effectiveness of parish ministry. Clergy couples and working spouses of pastors sometimes expect the appointment system to meet their needs before the needs of the congregation. Much of the time and energy of the church is being expended in attempting to get the institution to adjust to various individuals or classes of individuals.

The emergence and increasing importance of caucuses is a further example of the clericalization of our church. Meetings of the caucuses are often subsidized by national and conference funds. At caucus meetings, members plan strategies for getting "their" candidates elected to key positions in the church, to gain a larger share of denominational funds for more activities of the caucus, and to supress all criticism or rivalry from other caucuses. These caucuses are clergy dominated and, on the whole, concerned with issues of clerical power. The issues these groups raise tend to center on ways to make the institution provide recognition, positions, and status to people within the caucus. The transformation of the certified layworker into the diaconal minister is an example of the church's creating a category of ministry to provide recognition and status for a specific group. Such aspirations are understandable. The question of whether the changes in classification will increase the effectiveness of the church in proclaiming the gospel tends not to be given attention. Winning persons to Christ and ministering to the needs of the world are largely ignored in the debate of many clergy special interest groups. These priorities must be reversed; those who are called to be leaders in the Christian community must give their attention to serving, rather than to being served.

Maintaining Quality and Competence

The clergy, themselves, have the responsibility of maintaining a high level of quality and competence among their peers. It is the clergy who determine whom shall be admitted into the ministry. When a pastor is appointed to a church, the lay members are expected to accept and support him or her. If a pastor becomes lazy, incompetent, or immoral, the clergy have the responsibility to see that the individual makes appropriate behavioral changes or that disciplinary action is taken. The laypeople cannot act on their own. They can complain to denominational officials or, if they feel strongly enough, drop out of their local church.

While the vast majority of pastors are conscientious and competent, it is no secret that the clergy are also most reluctant to take action against one of their number unless his or her actions are flagrantly immoral or illegal. The *Discipline* provides a careful method for investigation and possible trial of clergy and lay members that is designed to protect the rights of the individual (see pars. 2620-2626). But we have all heard of shocking examples of how the clergy have failed to discipline or eject errant fellow clergy, resulting in a decline of respect for the ordained clergy by the laity and by the clergy for themselves. There are several reasons for this reluctance. Any professional group tends to protect its members. Furthermore, the church sees its task as being redemptive and assisting persons to reform. Pastors want to avoid being judgmental, and disciplining another pastor requires making extremely difficult judgments. There may be the feeling among the clergy that dealing with a problem pastor will cause a public scandal that will harm the church.

But the cover-up of a bad situation tends not to remain secret; it is like an untreated, festering sore that over the long term can do irreparable damage.

If The United Methodist Church is to have credibility in the larger society and if its clergy are to be effective and maintain integrity, the clergy must deal with their peers who betray their trust. They will also have to deal with those who, for whatever reason, are no longer effective. The church does not exist to give employment to the clergy, although we sometimes act as if that were its main task. Several concerned laypersons once called on a district superintendent to discuss a particularly inept pastor, whom they felt was exerting a negative influence on their church. The superintendent readily acknowledged that the laypersons were correct in their observations, but asked, "What are we going to do with him? He has only two or perhaps three appointments to serve before he can retire." One shocked lay member replied, "But what is he going to do to the churches he will serve in the next nine or ten years?" The district superintendent, by his response and subsequent action, made it clear that the pastor would be protected and appointed until retirement.

In our church, the Pastor-Parish Relations Committee, the district superintendents, and bishops are responsible for evaluating the effectiveness of the clergy. The *Discipline* states that pastoral effectiveness shall be evaluated annually by both the Pastor-Parish Relations Committee and the district superintendent (par. 422.1*b*). In actual practice, the superintendent plays the critical role in the process. It is essential that district superintendents develop a fair, clearly understood method for clergy evaluation and for securing direct feedback from both the pastor and the congregation concerning the minister's effectiveness.

The individual's ministry grows and develops through feedback. Corrective action can be initiated only if an accurate evaluation and diagnosis are made. Effective evaluation can assist the cabinet in better matching the pastor and the congregation. Evaluation, however, is not only a means for making better appointments, but also a way of developing more skillful pastors through accountability.

In the early days of Methodism in America, it was not unusual for persons to leave the ministry. Was it easier to change careers then than it is today? No, not really. There are plenty of opportunities for people with an education. The United Methodist Church must be willing to help persons leave the ministry when, for whatever reason, they are no longer effective. This must be done with as much care and understanding as possible, but it will still require difficult decisions. Presumably, this is why bishops and district superintendents are paid more than most of our other clergy—they must make difficult decisions. Persons who cannot make tough decisions, who place other concerns over the concerns about the integrity and the competence of the clergy, should not be appointed as district superintendents or elected as bishops. This may be the most difficult task the clergy will face, but it must be done if The United Methodist Church is to continue as a viable and effective institution in its third century. The clergy must become convinced that the church's mission is more important than their needs.

What Can Be Done?

The United Methodist appointive system is basically sound and has served the church well. Our system, like any other, is subject to abuse and manipulation by persons and groups seeking personal advantages. What can be done? Is it realistic to expect those who receive special benefits to change the system if such alterations threaten their benefits? We are convinced that such changes are not only necessary, but also possible.

There are two reasons for optimism. First, and most important, *the church throughout its history has had persons serving the cause of Christ without regard to self.* There have been leaders who have devoted themselves wholeheartedly to the church. Such persons have been a minority, but their impact on the life of the church is beyond calculation. In retrospect, we call such people saints, generally after they have been dead for some time. It is not unrealistic to assume that such persons may be found in The United Methodist Church today. They must set the tone for our clergy and receive the recognition and rewards of the system.

Second, *periods of difficulty tend to produce leaders who rise to the occasion and guide the institution through perilous times.* As the impact of the continued membership decline on the life of The United Methodist Church becomes more evident to greater numbers of people, the pressures to take corrective measures will increase. Business as usual will become unacceptable. Clerical leaders who do nothing but serve the interests of the clerical *status quo* will be rejected. Ways of operating, which serve vested interests instead of furthering the goals of the church, will not be tolerated. Change will not come without struggle and pain, but it must and will come.

In the light of this, three changes must occur. *United Methodists must understand the impact of some of our clergy deployment practices and realistically consider what must be done.* This means looking at hard facts, something that is neither easy nor pleasant. It is, however, a necessary beginning. *The clergy must accept their responsibility for ensuring that high standards are maintained.* Religious reform movements have tended to come at a time when the clergy were lax and developed a church structure that was self-serving. Temptation toward clericalism must be resisted. Finally, *the laity must become more assertive and refuse to tolerate clergy who are ineffective.* United Methdodist laypeople are much too passive and reluctant to challenge the clergy. Our structure does not encourage the laity to challenge the clergy, even when it is appropriate to do so. However, lay members can have more influence than most realize. These three steps would contribute significantly to the revitalization of the church.

Note

1. Lyle E. Schaller, *Understanding Tomorrow* (Nashville: Abingdon Press, 1976), p. 17.

Demand Leaders Instead of Managers

Chapter 5. The book of the Acts of the Apostles tells the story of the early church. The story is told, not by a description of interesting early church buildings or details of early procedures and organization, but rather by accounts of the early church's leaders. Acts is, for the most part, stories about leaders, such as Paul, Peter, Philip, Aquila, and Priscilla. In some organizations, truth is reached by a majority vote of the membership. In others, guidance is achieved by reference to constitution, by-laws, and organizational flow charts. The church, however, is historically, sometimes frightfully, dependent on its leaders. The truth of Christ comes through a person. It is personal. The church never outgrows the need for people who have the gifts and graces to lead us where we would not be able to go without their leadership. In Acts, early church leaders argue, debate, provoke controversy, encourage, rebuke, preach, suffer, and die for the sake of the Christ and his church. Today's church never marches beyond our leaders' vision.

The persons in key positions in The United Methodist Church today are primarily managers and not leaders. *Leaders* are persons with a vision that they are able to articulate. They can name the needs, desires, and hopes of the people. They have a charisma that inspires confidence. The people sense that the leader understands them and is working on their behalf. Because of this, they will follow a leader into new and uncharted paths.

Leaders establish new institutions; they revitalize and reform old ones. In the process, the established order may be drastically altered. Some existing institutions may be discarded to make way for new. Leaders tend to be controversial because they inevitably challenge existing social structures and accepted ways of doing things. They will inspire both love and enmity, but never indifference.

In contrast, *managers* accept the validity of the institutional *status quo* and give their attention to its maintenance. They see that everything is done correctly by the proper person and consistent with precedent. They write and revise policy manuals; the machinery is oiled and polished. In due course, the institution becomes an end in itself, rather than a means to serve a larger goal. Because managers assume the validity of the organization, they expect the constituents to be loyal to and supportive of the institution. This loyalty is expected even if the people do not feel that the institution is serving them and even if they are opposed to what the institution is doing.

Managers tend to become identified with an institution or that part of it for which they have responsibility. Their status in life is derived from their particular positions. A great deal of time and energy goes into defining and protecting one's area of responsibility or "turf." It does not matter whether the manager thinks of himself or herself as a political "liberal" or "conservative"; any change is threatening and will be resisted.

Every institution needs both leaders and managers; there are certain routine tasks that must be attended to. The problem has become that The United Methodist Church is dominated by managers. Maintaining the institution is their major concern; a great deal of energy is going into ensuring that the various parts are correctly organized and staffed by the appropriate number of designated categories of persons. More attention is being given to the form and composition of church organizations than to what these groups are actually accomplishing. Today the goal of these agencies is not to do but to be. The mere existence of the board or agency is considered to be a sufficient purpose for the board or agency. Our denomination thinks we have solved a given problem or met a particular need when an agency has been created and funded in the name of that problem or need.

Our church is overmanaged and underled. The rules are being followed, but there is no vision. Managers may be efficient in keeping the organizational wheels turning smoothly. However, leaders help people to see and to move toward significant goals.

What Jobs Are Considered Important?

A major indication of the managerial mentality prevalent in United Methodism is the importance given to the organizational form and work of the denominational agencies. There are 226 pages, or one-third of the text, of the current *Discipline* devoted to the organization and responsibilities of the general boards and agencies. It is safe to assume that this section is read only by that very small group of persons directly involved with the bureaucracy—those persons who derive their livelihood and their reason for being from these paragraphs in the *Discipline*.

The proportion of the *Discipline* devoted to the general agencies is an indication of the importance given to this part of the church. It is generally accepted, particularly among clergy, that the most significant positions are administrative and bureaucratic. These are perceived as being more desirable and as having more status than the local church pastors. The individual who moves from being a pastor of a local church to a position in a general agency is perceived as being promoted. The reverse is also true, as the person who leaves a bureaucratic staff job to become the pastor of a local church is perceived by other pastors as having been demoted. An illustration of the path of upward mobility was expressed by a young pastor serving his first appointment after graduating from theological seminary. He said, "After serving four or perhaps five charges, I'd like to become a district superintendent. After that, I hope to get a position on the staff of a general board." This minister reflected an attitude that is probably widely held but not often expressed so candidly.

It is a little difficult to understand why the administrative and bureaucratic positions are so highly prized. The salaries, except for the few highest positions, are not much better than those of a large number of local church pastors. When the value of the parsonage or housing allowance is taken into account, the actual income of many pastors would be equal to or higher than that of agency staff. The working conditions, such as regular hours and weekends free, are different from those in a parish. But like any job, there are negative aspects, such as extensive travel. One veteran agency staff member jokes, "These are good jobs for someone who does not get along with his wife."

Agency jobs are fewer in number than appointments to local churches, a factor that may contribute to their desirability. Persons in such posts may be perceived as exerting power, which is attractive to some people. However, the major reason is the overemphasis on a certain form of the institutional machinery as the reason for the church's existence. Those who manage and care for the machinery see themselves as and are perceived as doing the denomination's most important work. Recently, an annual conference held a pastors' school—a time for four hundred of the conference's clergy to meet, worship, and study. The bishop in that conference sent word that he would not be there, since he needed to attend a meeting of some national church committee on which he sits. The four hundred clergy surely got the bishop's message: Attending committee meetings is the real purpose of the church and its pastors.

To rectify past practices, which tended to exclude minorities and women, the denomination has been placing them in administrative and bureaucratic posts. A complicated quota system has been set up to ensure that women, ethnic minorities, persons with handicapping conditions, youth, young adults, and older adults will be represented as voting members of agency boards.[1] Executives are under considerable pressure to employ minorities and women.

Various caucuses lobby for this goal. It is a curious, almost tragic, circumstance that has led our women and minority members to accept the notion that the way for the church to rectify past inequities is to have more female and minority managers. Women and minorities have accepted the idea that the administrative and bureaucratic positions represent the highest level of attainment in the church and eagerly seek such posts.

The result of all this is that much time and energy goes into management of the institution. This is time and effort that is not going into preaching, winning persons to the gospel, building up congregations, and ministering to people. The sad fact is that the newest group (minorities and women) to move into leadership in the denomination has accepted some of the least desirable and most organizationally conservative values of the persons it is attempting to displace. Nothing is changing but the actors. Minority bureaucrats fail to increase our minority membership. People do not join a congregation saying, "Let's become United Methodists; they have an agency executive who is Hispanic." All too often, we have tried to attack the problem of the lack of ethnic evangelization by our church by removing effective ethnic pastors and moving them into positions that cut them off from the possibility of evangelizing anyone into the denominational structure beyond the local church.

The Rhetoric and the Reality

The self-image of most denominational officials is not that of institutional managers. Many of these people probably see themselves as leading the church into the battle against such evils as racism, sexism, agism, "handicapism" (an awkward contribution to the language invented by a church agency), and perhaps even other "isms" yet to be discovered. The rhetoric is that of bold leadership; the reality is that of control and maintenance of the institutional status quo at all levels of the connectional structure and suppression of alternative points of view. Managers know that there is no reason for their existence other than management of the existing machinery—so their vigilance over that machinery is fierce.

One need only look slightly below the surface to see the high priority placed on institutional maintenance. The test of loyalty for both the pastor and the congregation is whether the local church has paid all of the apportionments in full. The most detailed part of the annual report of each local church is that which gives the amount contributed to the various denominational causes. One type of information that many cabinets will have available at the time they meet to consider pastoral appointments is the amount of money apportioned to each charge during the preceding year and the total each paid. Pastors endeavor to persuade their congregations to pay these askings in full because of the possible effect on their next appointment.

Some will argue, "This is as it should be. Apportionments mean mission. In paying our apportionments, a congregation is moving outside its own selfish preoccupation with the pastor's salary and its internal needs and reaching out to serve the needs of others." This is not so. Apportionments represent agency salaries as much as they mean mission.

The money provided by the apportionments to the local churches are, in the main, used to pay the administrative expenses and the costs of the programs of the various denominational agencies, including subsidies to other churches and institutions. Many of these institutions are creations to meet the missional needs of an earlier day. Managers administer yesterday's decisions rather than lead us toward the creation of new institutions for new missional needs. The work of these groups is important and, in general, makes a contribution to the church and to the society. What is significant is that denominational officials indicate by their actions that it is the most important work that The United Methodist Church does and that it is the main means of mission. Keeping a steady flow of funds necessary to maintain the institution receives the highest priority. Despite the rhetoric, maintaining and managing the institution are what many officials feel is important.

Anything that threatens a part of the institution will be met with strong resistance. A recent example is the conflict between the General Board of Global Ministries and the independent Mission Society for United Methodists. The latter group wants to send missionaries but has encountered determined opposition. The underlying issue is a theological conflict over the nature of the church's mission, but the battle is being fought over bureaucratic authority. The General Board of Global Ministries claims it has been designated as the only missionary-sending agency by the General Conference. A number of the bishops have closed ranks with this board and have refused to appoint ordained ministers as staff or missionaries of the new independent agency; yet United Methodist clergy continue to be appointed to a variety of ecumenical and other, sometimes highly partisan, agencies. The difference in this instance is that an unofficial (but totally United Methodist) group is challenging a part of the institution. The new Mission Society is probably receiving some of the money that United Methodist people previously gave to the General Board of Global Ministries. The theological differences and the consideration of the most effective strategy for the church's mission are not being debated, while the struggle over bureaucratic turf continues. Here, again, we have an example of the prevailing attitude that makes maintenance of the institution paramount.

The manager may create the illusion of progress by tinkering with the ecclesiastical machinery. United Methodists are continually involved in this process, which has ranged from a general restructuring of the boards and agencies to reorganization of parts of the bureaucracy. Titles are altered, offices are moved across the hall or across the nation, and some of the actors are replaced, but relatively little actually changes because those in power will not surrender power easily.

The Desired Type of Leader

It is axiomatic that people get the kind of leaders they want. If this is the case, then United Methodists, and particularly the clergy, want managers who will care for and preserve the institution as it is. Managers tend the institutional machinery.

They are not threatening because they can be counted on to see that no radical changes will be made and that no tough choices will be faced. They may be dull, but they are comfortable. There will be some conflict, but it will be among people or groups who aspire to be the managers. We are told that there is nothing wrong with the machinery; we just need more female or black or conservative or liberal managers to run the machinery. The names on the doors change, but not the machinery; so nothing changes. The long-term result is a kind of institutional dry rot, which preserves the form after the strength has gone. The end result is, predictably, fatal.

Clergy tend to be comfortable with the denominational managers because they can be trusted to maintain the *status quo,* including protecting the status of the clergy. They are the main beneficiaries of the present machinery. The laypersons who are elected to denominational offices in both the annual conference and general church seem quickly to take on the perspective of the clergy. Despite the attempt of United Methodism to include laypersons in and on the various agencies, there is little evidence that it has had any effect in altering either the style or the direction of the denomination. The machinery is greater even than the laity; it turns all of us into managers.

While United Methodist laypeople will patiently tolerate managers as pastors of local churches, they welcome and respond to leaders. Laypersons want their church and their pastor to be effective. Members talking about their minister will often say, "He is a good man, but . . . " This is followed by some comment that reflects disappointment in a pastor who is uninspiring, unimaginative, and perhaps downright dull. The pastor is managing the local church, but not giving leadership, and the laity know it.

Dozens of congregations that are in trouble have been studied. These studies reveal that the three factors most important for revitalizing these dying congregations are *leadership, leadership, leadership.* In a declining congregation, the pastor appears to be depressed, impotent, immobile, not in control, a passive victim of the surrounding neighborhood or of the squabbling lay leaders or of the national bureaucracy; any alibi is given for the pastor's inability to see a vision of the church and to communicate that vision to the laity. When pressed to lead, these managers become rigidly legalistic, invoking one paragraph in the *Discipline* as their authority because they lack the leadership skills to convince, to convert, and to persuade. On the other hand, researchers can point with joy to a number of United Methodist congregations in which almost any obstacle has been overcome by the firm, visionary, enthusiastic leadership of a pastor who is a leader.

Take the case of the United Methodist church in Ossining, New York.[2] Three years ago their pastor, the Reverend Paul Bowles, was told, "We're old; we can't do much." Today the attitude is different.

For many years, the Ossining church had had no Sunday school. It had been thirty-five years since the last vacation Bible school. By 1983, there was barely a child left to light the candles on the altar. The church was empty and dying, the congregation depressed. Hopeless was the tenor of all conversations about the parish's future.

The pastor went to work. He called on everyone remotely related to the church and on many who were not. During that summer, he made 375 calls. He also spent time finding and training Sunday school teachers. When the prospective teachers were asked to name their greatest fear, they replied, "What if nobody comes?" But somebody did come; the day Sunday school opened, thirty children came.

Other things happened. The children brought brothers and sisters. Many had never attended Sunday school. Some parents followed. The youth group grew to twenty. Ten young people were confirmed in 1985 and twelve in 1986. There are two children's choirs. Last summer's vacation Bible school had ninety-two participants. The church is now a vital agent of ministry in families and the community.

Growing and effective congregations have ministers who are leaders, not managers. Vital denominations have leaders who lead, who chart new courses, and who inspire persons to follow, not simply to manage the institutional status quo. A strong leader releases strength in all of us. Too many clergy and laity today feel impotent, unable to move because they have been so effectively thwarted in their earnest efforts to get things moving. While we agree with most of Bishop Wilke's *And Are We Yet Alive?* in its enthusiastic call for renewal, we predict that such calls will produce only cynicism and despair if we fail to attend to the specific changes that are needed to turn our enthusiasm into the power to be effective. A revitalized United Methodism must place persons in official positions who are leaders and not simply managers, persons who have a vision of what the church can be and who inspire other people to risk making that vision a reality.

What Can Be Done?

If it is true that The United Methodist Church is dominated by managers instead of leaders, the question is what, if anything, can be done to change the situation? A change in the type and style of people now directing the denomination is not only possible, but also absolutely essential. Pastors and lay members can do several things to make a difference.

First and most important, *United Methodists must become more assertive.* We are too passive and accepting of what church officials do. There is an ethic at work that believes that one should not disagree or make waves. Such action is thought to produce conflict that will greatly damage the church. Mavericks are silenced or driven out. When this is combined with the feeling that persons in the local church cannot influence what the denominational agencies do, the result is a debilitating lethargy.

Furthermore, a kind of halo effect surrounds the minister. Some laypersons are reluctant to challenge the clergy because the laypersons seem to feel that to do so is almost like challenging God. The laity assume that the clergy—by training, vocation, or divine gifts—automatically know what is best for the church when, in reality, the clergy may be among the least able to look honestly at the church. This is particularly true in regard to denominational officials. United Methodists, both clergy and laity, must demand leaders and not simply managers who will maintain the institutional *status quo.*

Second, *United Methodist clergy and laity must look carefully at the process by which denominational officials are chosen.* The manner by which the selection is made can determine the type of person who will fill the position. The trend has clearly been toward an overt political process, in which persons openly campaign for a denominational office.

This is most obvious in, but not limited to, the election of bishops. The *Discipline* now permits the formal nomination of episcopal candidates (par. 506). Getting such a nomination is the equivalent of winning a primary election. This has resulted in campaign literature that requires the solicitation of funds from supporters or an investment by the candidate. It has also resulted in the exclusion of persons who might serve the church well, but who will not submit to the indignities of an ecclesiastical political campaign.

This present trend has shifted the emphasis from persons being called into the difficult role of leader to the finding of persons who can and are willing to put together the right coalitions to be elected. Caucuses and quotas produce managers, not leaders. The process by which persons attain church offices has contributed to the dominance of managers. People who openly campaign for an office in an institution can be counted on to maintain that institution or to make changes favorable to their supporters. They have already had to make so many compromises to be acceptable to so many different groups in their coalition that they can't remember what it means to lead.

Third, *United Methodists must be willing to find ways to ensure that the person selected to become church officials are leaders and not just managers.* Because an institution employs the type of leaders the constituents want, the people, if they desire, can have a different type of leader. When the institution is not doing well, the people tend to demand a change in leadership. The United Methodist Church has not been doing well. "If my company had lost 13 percent of its business in the last twenty years, I would be out of a job," one corporate vice president told us. Resistance to ideas for innovation can be expected from those who have presided over our current decline. It is time that the people called the church officials into account and demanded changes.

Notes

1. The 1984 *Discipline* provides that each annual conference shall nominate at least fifteen persons to a jurisdictional pool, out of which the managers of the various general agencies are elected. This pool is to contain clergy (including at least one woman), laywomen, laymen, and at least one person from each of the Asian American, Black American, Hispanic American, and Native American minority groups. Age categories include youth, young adults, and older adults. Finally, the nominees must include persons who have a handicapping condition. (Par. 805.*b*)

2. "Depressed Church Reaches Out for Cure." *People to People,* vol. 2, no. 1 (Nashville: The United Methodist Publishing House, 1986), p. 1.

Abolish the Minimum
Salary for Clergy

Chapter 6. The system of providing a minimum salary for all United Methodist pastors appointed to a charge may, at first, seem to have little relationship to church revitalization. But it is symptomatic of a major flaw within our present structure. This program, which has been known by several names, was first called the sustentation, then the minimum salary, and finally equitable salary. It was designed to provide a floor below which no minister's salary would be allowed to fall. The issue, however, is not primarily one of the pastor's income, but of the impact of subsidy on the clergy and on the local church. The minimum salary for clergy is only one form of subsidy the denomination provides to individuals, congregations, church-related institutions, and various other groups. The equitable salary program is an excellent example for review because it is denomination-wide and involves a large number of clergy and local churches. It is symptomatic of a kind of ecclesiastical system of subsidy that is having a debilitating effect on both pastors and congregations.

The Development of Minimum Salary

The present minimum salary program grew out of the mission program of the church. In the period before Methodist unification in 1939, the presiding elder (district superintendent) would apply to the annual conference or General Board of Mission for support for mission situations. These included churches that could not afford to support a minister, but in which the services of a pastor were needed. Mission funds supplemented the amount raised by the local congregation.

There developed in the late 1930s the concept that every pastor should receive a salary adequate to support him (and at that time it was almost universally a case of male pastors) and his family. The General Board of Lay activities, which included stewardship as a program emphasis, made support of the minister one of its goals. The *Discipline* of 1939 provided that each annual conference "may adopt a Schedule of Minimum Salary support for its Pastors."[1] To receive support, pastors were required to be serving full-time, but the amount provided could differ due to living conditions, number in the family, or any other reason.

Given the authority to subsidize clergy salaries, annual conferences proceeded to do so. The North Carolina Annual Conference was one of over forty to take such action. The Annual Conference Board of Lay Activities in 1940 asked the bishop to appoint a special committee to study the matter and make recommendations. This was done, and the following year a report was made. The committee stated that "adequate support did not mean a mere living just one jump ahead of the bread line . . . but enough to give sufficient security to make for efficiency on the part of the minister."[2] The report also pointed out that an automobile had become an absolute necessity for the minister. A salary schedule was set for clergy who were unmarried, married, and married with children. The funds were to be raised by a 2 percent apportionment on all money raised by each local church, except for buildings.

It should be noted that the minimum salary was inaugurated at the time when much discussion of a minimum hourly wage was taking place. The first minimum hourly wage was put into effect by the federal government on June 28, 1938. The church appears to have been influenced by events in the larger society.

With some minor modifications, the minimum salary

program has continued virtually unchanged, even though the originating assumptions of a mission oriented support program have been lost. Each annual conference sets the minimum amount a charge must pay the pastor. The figure differs in each annual conference; the exact amount for which a particular pastor is eligible is determined by a formula that takes into account his or her status and possible years of service. An elder in full connection receives a higher minimum salary than associate members, probationary members, or local (lay) pastors. In conferences that consider length of service, a minister with twenty-four years service may receive a salary as high as 21 percent greater than one with less than three years. The difference between the highest and lowest minimum salary in a particular annual conference may be as high as 50 percent; however, in most annual conferences the difference ranges from 10 to 30 percent.

If it is determined that a particular charge needs a pastor, but cannot, after every effort has been made, provide the required minimum salary, the annual conference makes up the difference. Most annual conferences have a limit on the amount a charge may receive. The funds providing the salary supplement continue to be provided by an apportionment levied on each local church.

What Went Wrong?

The minimum salary program is based on two assumptions. The first is that an ordained minister could be sent to a charge too small to afford to employ a pastor, but where one was needed. It was hoped that the pastor might cause the church to develop to the point at which a subsidy would no longer be required. The second assumption was that minimum salary would guarantee that each minister would receive a modest, but adequate, income no matter where in the annual conference he or she might be appointed. However, the minimum salary program has not worked out as it was hoped. There are three reasons for this.

First, *instead of providing a floor below which clergy salaries should not fall, the minimum salary has too frequently been interpreted as a ceiling or as the appropriate compensation for the pastor.* Congregations look at the amount set by the annual conference and conclude that is about what a pastor should be paid. The currently popular term, "equitable salary," may further convey to the congregation that this figure is a fair salary, particularly if the membership is small and having a difficult time making ends meet.

Some congregations do not want to be known as a minimum salary church because this label calls attention to the fact that they are paying their pastor only what is required. To avoid what may be perceived as a stigma, they set their salaries slightly above the required minimum. This probably accounts for the fact that in many annual conferences 30 to 50 percent of the pastors' cash salaries will tend to be clustered around the required minimum salary, varying by only two or three thousand dollars. Thus the minimum salary program may actually depress clergy income by making a low level of compensation acceptable.

Second, *the formation of charges with too few members to employ a full-time pastor is encouraged.* Circuits that provide both an adequate work load and adequate compensation wish to divide so that each church may have its own minister. To do so, each church may pay a salary at or near the minimum. The churches may enjoy the status of being station appointments, but the ministers may be frustrated because they do not have enough to do. Each church will have to increase its expenditures for the minister's salary, but because each is supporting a pastor, the ministers now may actually be receiving less than their predecessors, who served a circuit.

Furthermore, the availability of minimum salary funds protects both local and denominational leaders from having to make tough decisions about a congregation's future. It is easier to subsidize a church than to make the arrangements for it to become part of a circuit. Such an action means change, which will be resisted by some. It also means assisting the congregations in facing up to their responsibility for ministry and outreach in the present, a task that is never easy.

Third, and most important, *the minimum salary tends to shift some of the responsibility for ministerial support from the local church to the denomination.* The fact that the pastor's salary comes out of the congregation's collection plate, either the one he or she is serving or from other local churches, is overlooked. It may not be realized that funds provided by the denomination originate in the congregations. When the clergy receive part of their salary from the denomination, the tendency is to perceive the annual conference as the employer. This creates a dependent relationship between the pastor and the annual conference. The action of the annual conference in setting the minimum salary levels can be more important to the minister than an increase in worship attendance in the local church.

Problems with Subsidy

Subsidy, even when it is essential, always has some negative consequences. There are instances in which financial support would be provided, but there are problems that must be recognized. The church has a long tradition of giving to support a wide range of ministries and to provide for those in need. This can be an appropriate response for those who follow Christ. The scriptures remind us that "it is more blessed to give than to receive" (Acts 20:35), a statement that has more truth than is often realized. While there always have been and will continue to be ministries needing financial aid from the denomination, the negative consequences of such aid must be recognized.

One negative consequence is the tension between the grantor and the recipient. This is due to the fact that the agency providing the funds is in a position of power. The individual or group receiving the subsidy, by the fact that financial support is needed, is reminded of an inherent weakness. The need for financial support constantly calls attention to weakness and is a source of irritation. No matter how gracious and understanding the granting agency may be, it is always in a position to discontinue the subsidy. The one thing that the person or agency providing the subsidy cannot expect in return is love. Resentment and animosity are more likely to be the results of long-term subsidization. Any mission board continually has to deal with the tensions and conflicts that occur between the granting agency and the recipients of funds. These tensions and conflicts need not become destructive, but they are inherent parts of the relationship when subsidies are involved.

A second negative consequence is the dependency subsidization develops. The longer outside funds are provided, the more the recipient comes to depend on their continuance. The group receiving the subsidy comes not only to expect it, but also to perceive it as their right. As dependency increases, local initiative decreases. It is always easier to accept outside help than to raise the necessary funds locally. The dependency produced by long-term subsidization results in a congregation that looks to outside sources of support instead of reaching out to new people and increasing the number of persons who participate.

An example of the negative impact of subsidization is the membership trend among United Methodism's black constituency. The recent revelation that the number of black members barely increased, despite the denomination's emphasis on ethnic ministries and that the numbers of black members in several other predominantly white denominations had surpassed those in the United Methodist Church, came as a shock.[3] The most disturbing aspect of this information is that it came after two decades during which the church had been putting millions of dollars into subsidies for ethnic churches and projects. It is impossible to get an exact figure, but the total would be substantial. The general boards and agencies have, over a long period, provided substantial amounts to minority churches and causes from their regular budgets; this would include such items as the Minority Group Self-Determination Fund administered by the General Commission on Religion and Race, which for the quadrennium 1985–1988 is budgeted at one million dollars per year.[4]

There have been at least four church-wide emphases (The Temporary General Aid Fund, 1964–1968; The Racial Witness Relief Fund, 1964–1968; The Fund for Reconciliation, 1968–1972; and The Ethnic Minority Local Church, 1980–1988) that have focused on ethnic ministries. The expenditure of large sums has not resulted in revitalized local churches and increased outreach to minority people, but instead has contributed to the development of an increasingly dependent constituency, who tend to perceive continued subsidization as an entitlement. Well intentioned efforts seem to be achieving the exact opposite of what was intended.

The church, like many other institutions in American society, tends to attempt to solve problems by appropriating funds. Giving money is, after all, the easiest thing to do. Furthermore, providing money is a convenient way of dealing with any feelings of guilt.

For the local church, the problem is people first and money second. Subsidies may be needed in some situations, such as when a new congregation is being developd, but it is difficult to provide support over the long term without negative consequences. The length of time the subsidy will be provided must be carefully defined on the basis of how it can aid the mission of the church. Subsidies must be periodically evaluated as to effectiveness and must be terminated after a stated period of time. The inherent problems must be recognized and addressed, particularly when a local church is the recipient. Congregations, like individuals, have a tendency to become self-centered and self-satisfied. Support from the denomination lessens the incentive to reach out and bring new persons into the group.

Church Membership and Ministers' Salaries

The ministry is not and has never been a highly paid profession. The individual whose objctive is financial reward is neither likely to enter the ministry nor should. When compared to persons in other service occupations, the United Methodist minister tends to be paid less than some and more than others. The ministry, like almost all service professions, will pay substantially less than law, dentistry, and medicine. But the ministry compares favorably with other service professions and even more so when benefits are taken into account. For example, the average (mean) minimum salary for ministerial members of fifty-six annual conferences is slightly over $15,000; this figure does not include such benefits as pension, insurance, and housing, most of which are tax exempt. The minimum salary for clergy, when the various benefits are included, exceeds the compensation of social workers, registered nurses, school teachers, physicians' assistants, police officers, fire fighters, and military personnel.

Clergy salaries are not determined by what persons in other occupations make, by the importance of the minister's task, nor by the amount of formal education required for ordination. The pastor's salary will be directly related to the strength of the charge to which he or she has been appointed. The larger the number of contributing members, the greater the potential for the congregation to provide the necessary funds for the operation of the local church.

There is a high correlation between the average attendance at the principal service of worship and the pastor's salary. An examination was made of the average worship attendance and the pastor's salary of ten annual conferences in different parts of the country. This indicated that the proportion of churches with an average worship attendance of 150 or more approximately equaled the number of ministers' salaries, not including benefits, of $20,000 or more.

The point is not the obvious one that the greater the number of worshipers, the larger the offering. The point is that *the pastor and the congregation must look to their own resources to develop and support their ministry, rather than to some denominational agency for subsidies or for a more desirable appointment.* The pastor who is ready for a greater salary—that is, a larger congregation—instead of building one, now expects the bishop to appoint him or her to such a church. Like the congregation that accepts minimum salary subsidies year after year, the tendency is to look to the denomination to meet the expectations. When the resources of an outside agency are available, they will be utilized; people and institutions will take the easiest paths. This also means that they will be less inclined to work hard at developing the local congregation, at reaching out and bringing new persons into the fellowship.

The issue is one of attitude, how the pastor perceives his or her ministry both in the present and in the future. Significant progress would be made toward church revitalization if the ministers viewed success as developing their present congregations, rather than looking to the denomination to provide what they perceive as a more desirable appointment. Abolishing the minimum salary would be a significant step toward achieving this goal.

Needed Results

To suggest any change in the minimum salary program, other than raising the amount, is not likely to be popular; to suggest that it be abolished will be considered heresy. Note that it is not being suggested that mission programs be abandoned or that every local chuch needs to be self-supporting. There are situations in which a United Methodist witness and ministry is needed and where, for any number of reasons, the local resources do not exist to provide the necessary support. New congregations need assistance until they can become established. Isolated rural communities in which there is no other church or certain inner city communities in which the level of social disorganization is high may require outside support.

What we are suggesting is that regular long-term subsidization, which causes congregations and pastors to look to the denomination for support instead of reaching out to people and, thereby, increasing the support base in their communities, be discontinued. Equitable salary is the place to begin. This will take some degree of adjustment by both congregations and pastors. Small stations would have to share a pastor as they become part of a circuit. Greater emphasis on lay ministry, a prominent part of early Methodism, would be needed. Congregations would have to make a greater effort to win some of the unchurched in their communities in order to have enough people to survive as an institution. Both old and new members would benefit from the process. Pastors would begin to understand that their future, as well as their present, ministry is directly linked to their ability to witness effectively in their community and to win persons to the church. The abolition of the minimum salary program is one of the few legislative changes suggested in this book; it is a change that could have beneficial results among our pastors and churches.

Notes

1. *Doctrines and Discipline of The Methodist Church 1939* (New York: The Methodist Publishing House, 1939), par. 816.

2. *Journal of Proceedings* (the Third Session of the North Carolina Annual Conference, 1941), p. 87.

3. "Ethnic Membership Barely Grows in 'Priority' Decade," *The United Methodist Reporter* (January 31, 1986), p. 1

4. *Forty-fourth Annual Report of The General Council on Finance and Administration of The United Methodist Church* (Evanston, Ill.: General Council on Finance and Administration, 1983), p. 147.

Insist That the Clergy Teach in the Parish

Chapter 7. Many of us came into The United Methodist Church in a world very different from the one in which we now live. It appeared to be a world of sure values, a coherent world view—at least among white, middle-class Americans, the Americans who formed the majority of United Methodism. Above all, as mainline Protestants, we felt as if we were in control. At one time, we Methodists were the largest denomination of the Protestant majority. This was "our" country, the place in which the Wesleyan revival had experienced its most astounding success. We were called, with much justification, "the most American of all American churches." We, therefore, assumed that the surrounding culture affirmed and confirmed our values. We felt that we did not have to work too hard to train our young in the Christian ethic; we did not have to belabor the distinctive quality of the Christian vision. After all, this was "our" country. Having a church within a democratic American environment was formation enough.

If we were ever justified in holding such a view of the church and its surrounding culture, few Christians believe that we can hold it today. We have learned, quite painfully, that our youth will not grow up Christian, will not embrace this faith by simply watching television and living in the "right" neighborhood. Powerful social forces are at work in us and in our world, necessitating a renewed commitment to the task of Christian formation if we are to survive as a particular people in contemporary America.

Actually, this is much the same conclusion as that reached by John Wesley in eighteenth-century England. The Wesleyan revival was never a matter of simply attracting great numbers of people by great preaching. Methodists were "methodical" in their approach to Christian renewal. They knew that the church must devise methods to insure that latter-day disciples understood the cost of discipleship and were willing to pay. The Conference was the agency Wesley devised to enable the Christian pastors, teachers, and people to define the faith and to guide their ongoing communal life. The agenda of Wesley's Conferences focused on the basic questions of:

1. What to believe (the understanding of the gospel);
2. What to teach (the proclamation of the gospel);
3. What to do (the activation of the gospel).[1]

While the Christian faith may be simple to accept, it is not easy to understand. Religion is necessarily complex because it deals with values by which the individual finds meaning in life and standards of conduct. To understand the Christian faith still requires conscious and disciplined effort. The importance of instructing people in the faith is illustrated by Jesus' telling his followers to make disciples by "teaching them to observe all that I have commanded you" (Matt. 28:20).

Many people in the contemporary church, including many committed Christians, do not have an adequate understanding of their faith. Biblical illiteracy, of the sort that John Wesley would have deplored, is rampant. This occurs despite the fact that the Bible is central to United Methodism's understanding of the faith. This lack of understanding comes at a time when the level of formal education of United Methodist clergy and of most of the laity has never been higher.

People do not become Christians by doing what comes naturally. The way of Christ requires conversion, discipline, formation, a lifetime of response, and constant attention.

Wesley knew this. His was not only an experienced "religion of the warm heart," but a religion of the mind as well. Wesley had little patience with preachers or society members who would not devote themselves to constant study, continual formation, and a lifetime of disciplined growth—*sanctification*. There are some Christian denominations that are suspicious of intellectual endeavor, seeing study, reflection, and the application of reason as threats to faith. These churches inculcate sets of rigid beliefs and narrow principles into their members. The United Methodist Church has never been afraid of intelligent examination, exploration, and study of the faith. Wesley believed that such study made better Christians, and Christian education was a primary focus of his ministry. Therefore, in the Wesleyan tradition the pastor is always the chief Christian educator in the congregation.

Why Knowledge of the Faith Is Poor

No one single factor has caused the lack of knowledge about the Christian faith, characteristic of this generation of church members. Instead, a combination of factors has brought about the present situation.

The church now provides a wider variety of curricula, but far fewer regular opportunities for lay people to study than a generation ago. The Wednesday evening prayer meeting and Bible study has, for the most part, long vanished from United Methodist churches. Attendance at this service helped the participants become familiar with the scriptures. Likewise, the now defunct Sunday evening service was a time when pastors often preached a special series of sermons on a book of the Bible. The Sunday evening service was more often than not a learning as well as a worship experience.

The Sunday school (some establishment types persist in calling it "church school," but it is time to acknowledge what everyone knows: the semantic innovation never caught on) which has been the major teaching activity of the church, has had a long-term decline. In the period from 1974 to 1984, the total enrollment in the church's Sunday schools decreased every year. The total decline during the decade was 14 percent. The adult enrollment also decreased every year, but at a slower rate. The 1984 figure was 5 percent less than that in 1974. A smaller proportion of United Methodist children and youth are participating in the Sunday school than was the case a generation ago.

Part of the decline in religious knowledge is due to changes in the larger society. The increasing concentration of the population in urban areas has provided people with more options for their free time. The church simply has greater competition for the members' time and attention. The local church, and particularly the adult Sunday school class, is less the center of the individual's social life than was the case in the past.

Despite the decrease in some of the traditional educational activities of the church, people are still interested in learning about their faith. Each year every local church reports the average attendance in short-term classes conducted in that congregation. Every year during the past decade, this figure increased. In 1974, the average attendance in short-term classes was slightly over one million; in 1984 it was a million and a third. This represents a gain of 29 percent. This increase may show that the traditional Sunday school format is giving way to short-term study groups. Without a doubt, it shows that a substantial number of United Methodist people are obviously interested in learning about their faith.

Why Pastors Do Not Teach

Teaching has not been one of the customary activities for large numbers of United Methodist pastors. There are several reasons why this has been the case. One primary reason is the particular history of Methodist clergy. The Methodist movement began as a revival. It had a strong emphasis on preaching and calling people to repentance. Nurture and discipline were provided in the small groups, the classes, and the bands, which were led by laypersons. John Wesley provided materials to be studied and expected that they would be used by the local groups.

The Methodist pastor was an itinerant. His appointment was to a circuit. While the traveling preacher was moving from church to church, the day-to-day oversight of the congregation was the responsibility of the local preacher, who was a layperson. Even after the time when clergy appointments tended to be for two or three years in the same charge, a large proportion of clergy served a circuit of two or three churches. Preaching in more than one community every week or alternating between communities every other week was not conducive to systematic, ongoing teaching.

The lack of emphasis on teaching is seen in the historic examination for a minister's admission into full connection of an annual conference. Of the nineteen questions, only one makes any reference to teaching. This asks, "Will you diligently instruct the children in every place?" (*Discipline,* par. 424.14). In listing the pastor's responsibilities, the *Discipline* states that the minister is "to give oversight to the total educational program of the church and encourage the distribution and use of United Methodist literature" (par. 439.3) and "to instruct candidates for membership . . ." (par. 439.4).

One might assume that the increased educational requirements for the clergy would have resulted in an increased interest in teaching. United Methodist clergy are now expected to have completed four years of college and three years of theological school. The charge is sometimes made that this training produces pastors who are too academic. In fact, there is virtually no expectation that the clergy will engage in serious teaching by either the denominational leaders, clergy peers, or laypeople. The annual report contains the number of weddings, funerals, and baptisms conducted. It lists the number of members gained and lost and average attendance at worship, and it shows the amount of money the congregation contributed to virtually every denominational cause. It does *not* ask if the minister has done any teaching during the past year.

Teaching requires time and disciplined effort. It is hard work. The average pastor is busy and is not likely to expend the effort on a task that receives no recognition from either peers or superiors and is not demanded by the local church members. Hence, energies will be directed to those tasks for which the minister perceives there will be some pay-off for his or her efforts.

Certain aspects of theological education may tend to make the pastor shy away from serious teaching in the local church. One is the increasing sophistication of the seminary subjects the pastor has studied. Some ministers may feel that it is impossible to instruct the laypeople at the level the ministers have attained. This is particularly true in biblical studies. Many pastors seem to feel that their understanding of the scriptures, particularly the historical-critical method they learned in seminary, has created an almost unbridgeable gulf between them and their lay members. One pastor, commenting on his local church, said, "I just could not teach my people the understanding of the Bible that I have learned in seminary." He chose to avoid the subject altogether.

Another factor that may hinder the minister's willingness to teach is the current emphasis on pastoral counseling and clinical pastoral education. This discipline has contributed much to the minister and has enhanced his or her ability to assist persons in dealing with problems and the crises that occur in life. However, the person whose primary interest is in pastoral counseling is less likely to want to instruct the laypersons in cognitive matters, such as Bible and theology, since counseling has put so much stress on psychological and experiential insights rather than on cognitive insights. For some clergy, a devotion to the psychological processes can be a way of not having to deal with the difficult biblical, theological, and ethical questions the Christian faith would have us confront.

Why the Clergy Should Teach

Regular teaching by the clergy would be a significant step toward the revitalization of The United Methodist Church. There are at least three specific benefits. First, a number of laypersons would become better informed about their faith and about their church. Obviously, this would not be a large group, because the average pastor could teach only a limited number of people.

Second, the teaching pastor would provide a model for laypersons to emulate. By the pastor's teaching regularly, he or she would communicate to the lay members that the church was convinced that understanding the scriptures and the faith was important. Laypersons, following their pastor's example, would be encouraged to engage in serious study. The pastor's teaching would also model good pedagogical methods for the lay teachers within the congregation. While the Sunday school is not the only occasion for a pastor to teach, one of the characteristics of a growing Sunday school is that the pastor is a regular teacher. A pastor's presence in any activity is always a signal to the congregation of the importance the pastor places on that activity.

Third, preparation of courses would be a valuable form of continuing education for the clergy. The United Methodist Church has in recent years expressed increased concern over the need for its ministers to update continually their knowledge and to improve their skills. Every pastor is required to engage in some appropriate form of continuing education annually. The denomination, as well as many local churches, provides funds for this purpose. Continuing education courses on teaching methods could be provided, but the best training for the minister is preparing and teaching a particular subject.

The crisis of faith, which is felt by many modern people, is, in great part, a crisis of meaning. Over a decade ago, Dean Kelley, in *Why Conservative Churches Are Growing,* argued that some churches grow because they take seriously the intellectual function of the church. They explain to people "the meaning of life in ultimate terms."[2] People cannot live without meaning, without some belief structure that gives life coherance and substance. If our church neglects the intellectual task, we can be sure that people will search elsewhere.

We are convinced that there is a desire among laypersons for serious study of religious subjects. The number of adult courses offered by the public schools and community colleges is substantial. Subjects will range from bicycle repair to Russian writers. Public institutions rarely offer courses on religious subjects. The most significant issues, such as ultimate values, matters dealing with the meaning of life and death, and ethical decisions, can be seriously studied only within the church. If The United Methodist Church is to experience revitalization, the clergy must give leadership by dealing with these issues in greater depth than can be done in the twenty-minute sermon on Sunday morning. Regular, substantive courses taught by pastors is the way to begin.

Notes

1. *The Book of Discipline of The United Methodist Church 1984* (Nashville: The United Methodist Publishing House, 1984), par. 67.
2. Dean Kelly, *Why Conservative Churches are Growing* (New York: Harper & Row, 1972), p. 37.

Simplify the Local Church Structure

Chapter 8. The sign out front identified the beautiful little building as Shady Grove United Methodist Church. The church was a building of no more than three or four rooms. (Shady Grove had fewer than one hundred members.) Proudly displayed in the front hallway of the church was a large chart entitled "Officers and Organizations," which listed all the officers of the congregation, including chairperson of the Administrative Board, chairperson of the Council on Ministries, chairperson of the Board of Trustees, and so on. The vast array of boards and committess, all interlocked through various lines of accountability, presented an impressive flow-chart of organization at Shady Grove. Upon closer examination of the chart, we noted that someone named Emma Smith held no less than *six* major offices of the church and was a member of *eight* boards and committees. A total of about twenty names appeared on the chart! There is nothing amiss in a small congregation being led by about a fifth of its total membership. Nor is it strange that one person, Emma Smith, is the main force at Shady Grove. What is strange is to have a small, family-like congregation (a large proportion of United Methodist churches) depicted by a flow-chart as if it were General Motors!

Each United Methodist church has its organization determined by the General Conference. The details of the required structure of the local church, including the required officials and committees and their responsibilities, are specified in the *Discipline*. This book is published every four years and mandates the polity for all parts of the denomination. The uniformity of organization, which the *Discipline* maintains, is an important aspect of United Methodism's connectional system; the *Disicipline* is responsible for the degree of consistency that is found among the congregations of the denomination.

The way in which the local church is organized is of the utmost importance because it determines to a great degree those items to which the congregations will give attention. If the *Discipline* mandates a particular committee and defines its area of responsibility, a large number of local churches will attempt to follow the instructions set by the General Conference. To a greater degree than is probably realized, the program emphasis and the issues the congregation addresses will be determined by the required organization.

We contend that there are two serious, inter-related problems with the structure of the local church. The first is the sheer complexity that results in too much time and energy expended in keeping the ecclesiastical machinery operating. The second is that the primary purpose of much of the organization, which the local church is mandated to have, is designed to meet the needs of the denominational boards and agencies, rather than those of the people in the congregation. These two matters must be addressed if revitalization is to occur within The United Methodist Church.

An Increasingly Complex Structure

There was a time not too long ago when the structure of a local church was relatively simple. The early years of the Methodist Church, which had been created by the unification of the three branch Methodist denominations in 1939, was such a time. The *Discipline* of 1940 provided for Quarterly Conferences to be the governing body. The group elected the officers, including Stewards, Trustees, Communion Stewards, Treasurer, Financial Secretary, and the Superintendent of the Church School. The administration of the local church was the responsibility of the Official Board. This body had the authority to elect up to eight optional committees if it was deemed advisable; these were evangelism, stewardship, temperance, music, parsonage, property, world peace and good literature.[1] These committees were optional and established only if the Quarterly Conference deemed any necessary.

What is significant about the local church organization of that period is not that it provides a minimum of organization, but that it assumed that the pastor and the congregation were capable of determining and implementing the program and ministry of the local church. Several committees were listed, but these were organized only if needed. Most of these dealt primarily with matters of concern to the local church. Three of the optional committees—evangelism, temperance, and world peace—also had parallel general agencies with the same areas of responsibility.

By 1952, the local church structure was still fairly simple, but more was being required. There was still a required first and fourth quarterly conference with the latter being the annual business meeting. An official board continued to be the administrative body; the several optional committees included nominations, pastoral relations, records and history, parsonage, and social and economic relations. A Board of Trustrees was responsible for the property. The *Discipline* stated, "Four phases of activity are essential to the spiritual life and ministry of every local church: evangelism, education, missions and finance."[2] A commission to deal with each of these areas was required in every local church. A Commission on Worship and a Commission on Social and Recreational Activities were optional.

What is important about the required program organization of this period is not only its simplicity, but also that it focused on matters essential to the local church. Evangelism was listed first. Winning converts had a high priority. Education was named next, indicating the importance of nurturing persons in the faith. Missions showed the need for the congregation to participate in outreach beyond the local community. Finally, funds were essential to the operation of the church. Three of the four required commissions (evangelism, education, and missions) had general boards with the same area of responsibility. The trend toward parallel structures at all levels of the denomination was taking shape.

Over the years, the structure of the local church has become larger and more complex. With the Methodist–Evangelical United Brethren merger in 1968, the Council on Ministries concept was introduced. This concept (first called the Program Council) had its origin in the EUB church. It represented an attempt to meet a need for a wholistic ministry and to broaden the group making program decisions, which had been the prerogative of the financial agencies. Various changes were made during the merger process. For the local church, it resulted in the creation of a body to "consider, develop, and coordinate goals and program proposals for the church's mission" (*Discipline*, par. 257).

The general oversight of administration and program is assigned to the administrative board. In addition to a board of trustees, three administrative committees (nominations, finance, and pastor-parish relations) are mandated.

To carry on the program of the local church, it is recommended that ten work areas (Christian unity and inter-religious concerns, church and society, education, evangelism, higher education and campus ministry, missions, religion and race, status and role of women, stewardship, and worship) be set up. It is also recommended that four age-level and specialized-ministry coordinators (children's ministries, youth ministries, adult ministries, and family ministries) be elected. These are in addition to the traditional local church organizations, such as the United Methodist Women, United Methodist Men, the United Methodist Youth Fellowship, and the Sunday school.

In 1980, some sanity prevailed when the General Conference, largely through the efforts of persons concerned with small parishes—the majority of United Methodist churches—authorized a simpler organizational form. This consists of an adminstrative council, a board of trustees, and the three administrative committees but combines the ten work areas into two (nurture, and membership and outreach). This action actually recognized that a majority of local churches (like Shady Grove) had too few members to have the required large structure and thus were forced to ignore it. It is stated, however, that where resources permit, the larger plan is the preferred model for organization.

The local church organization is based on two implicit principles. The first is coordination. Every activity is supposed to be coordinated with every other activity. It is almost as if there were a conscious attempt to prevent anyone or any group from doing anything, unless their activity were coordinated with every other activity. The result can be delays and a loss of momentum. One layperson commented, "we discuss the same issues in the work area on education, in the council on ministries, and finally in the administrative board. The repetition is boring."

Certain officers—such as the lay leader, the lay delegates to annual conference, and the president of the United Methodist Women—are members of several other bodies. Such persons, if they are conscientious, spend a great deal of time attending meetings. Lay members do not have unlimited time to give to the church. The present structure is not using their time most effectively.

The second principle is involvement of the maximum number of people in as many decisions as possible. The result of this practice is that a large number of people are expending an amount of time and energy in keeping the local church machinery running that is incommensurate with the results being achieved. The proper procedures tend to become an end in themselves, rather than a means to an end.

United Methodists seem to believe that participating in the administration of the local church is the primary task of the Christian. Of course, some administrative tasks are essential and need to be performed efficiently, but such tasks are a means rather than an end. Witnessing to one's faith is exciting; committee work on maintaining the institution can be dull and boring. A reason so many laypersons have little enthusiasm for the work of the church or get such little satisfaction from their efforts is that their time and talents are used in keeping the ecclesiastical machinery operating.

To Serve the General Agencies

The question United Methodists ought to be asking is why the *Discipline* continues to set forth as the desirable organizational model a large and complex structure, which a large majority of local churches do not follow and have never followed. The fact is that the general boards and agencies tend to have a dominant influence on what goes into the *Discipline*. It is no secret that most general agencies establish a task force on general conference legislation to draft their quadrennial desired "mandates." This includes the material on the structure of the local church. Thus the organization of the congregation does not reflect the needs or interests of the parish. The structure is, instead, designed to serve the program and promotional needs of the general agencies.

Bureaucracy expands not only by employing more staff at the national level, but also by getting the church to require parallel organizations at all levels of the denomination. A classic example of the way bureaucracy expands can be noted in the development of the General Commission on the Status and Role of Women. In 1972, this commission was established by the General Conference for four years, 1973–1976. Four years later, the 1976 *Discipline* provided for a Commission on the Status and Role of Women but did not give it a time limit. It was clear that there was a new star in the bureaucratic firmament. That year, the influence of this agency was increased by the requirement for each of the annual conferences to establish a Commission on the Status and Role of Women. Four years later, in 1980, this organization was given a greater degree of permanence by the statement that there will be a standing General Commission on the Status and Role of Women. Finally, in 1984, twelve years after the original commission had been given a temporary charter, the *Discipline* provided for a work area on the status and role of women in the local church. The establishment of parallel organizations in all levels of the church was then complete, a textbook case of an agency taking on a life of its own.

The *Discipline* makes it quite clear that the various units within the local church are to look to the corresponding general agency for guidance. The local church council on ministries "shall receive and, where possible, utilize resources for missions, provided by the District, Annual, Jurisdictional, Central, and General Councils on Ministries, boards, and agencies, and shall coordinate these resources with the church's plan for ministries" (*Discipline,* par. 257). The chairpersons of the various work areas are instructed to be guided by the corresponding general agency. A typical example of such instruction:

> The work area chairperson of higher education and campus ministry shall keep the Council on Ministries aware of higher education concerns and provide locally for the promotion and support of the interest of higher education and campus ministry in accordance with the programs of the Annual Conference and the General Board of Higher Education and Ministry. (*Discipline,* par. 261.5a)

The local group, therefore, is the creature of the corresponding general agency.

The problem is not with the work that the general agencies do; much is worthwhile. The problem is that a large proportion of the structure of the local church is designed to serve the interests of the general agencies, not necessarily the mission of the local church. These interests may or may not coincide with the interests and needs of the congregation. An examination of the recommended organization of the local church clearly reveals that the work areas are parallel to those of the general agencies. These are to be the local outlets or branch offices of the general agencies. The agencies need persons to whom they can send material, and a chairperson of a parallel committee in each local church fills this need.

This system of organization has two negative effects. First *it communicates to the local people that the really important ministry of the church is "out there" some place, not in the congregation or community.* With the overemphasis on the work of the general agencies, what the people and the pastors are doing in the local church is downgraded. This is one of the reasons why so many pastors place such great importance on the work of the general agencies and actually depreciate their own tasks. Second, *the agenda for the local church is set by church bureaucrats who have a particular interest and area of responsibility.* This relieves the pastor and the local leaders from facing the significant issues and needs in their community. They may complain about the program handed down from Nashville or New York or from the annual conference staff, but passively accept it. By following the program from the denominational agencies, they can have the sense of performing properly while not having to face certain issues in the local church and community.

Next Steps

The form of organization of a local church can be either an advantage or a handicap. Bishop Richard B. Wilke correctly described the present state of affairs, "Our energies and resources are expended internally. The machinery of the church receives unbelievable attention; we scurry about oiling the wheels of the organizational structure."[3] The organization has become a handicap to the creation of a vital church. The situation is particularly insidious because the goals of the various local committees, although often secondary, nevertheless are worthwhile. However, they assume a constituency that has been converted and is committed to the Christian faith, something that does not necessarily exist. Furthermore, they require so much time in complex administration that even the goals themselves become fuzzy.

Three things need to be done. First, United Methodists must realize that the structure of the church is to enable the gospel to be preached and ministries to be practiced. Because these functions are primarily carried out in the parish, organization at all levels should enhance the work of the congregation.

Second, the primary responsibility for the program and ministry of the local church must rest with the congregation, not with the church bureaucracy. The leaders of the denomination must trust the people with the gospel. It is ironic that at a time in which the educational level of the clergy, and probably that of the laity, has never been higher, the patronizing instructions given to the local church, concerning how they should be organized and what they should do, have also reached an all-time high.

What would happen if congregations were left to determine how they would witness and minister? It is likely that issues of importance in the local church and community would be addressed. Whatever happened would be done because the people felt it was important. The people would have a high sense of ownership for the church program, which does not exist today. Detailed, patronizing legislation from on high is a short-cut for convincing people that certain needs ought to be met, an attempt by the national church to achieve through the law what only the gospel can do. We must trust the power of the gospel to create, at the local church level, the sort of church the gospel demands.

Third, the system of having a local unit to parallel the various parts of the church bureaucracy needs to be discontinued. While we do not intend to downgrade the importance of the work of the denomination's agencies, the present structure makes the work of the local churches appear to be of secondary importance to that of the general agencies. This is exactly the opposite of the way the denomination should operate. The primary function of the general agencies is to enhance the work of the local churches. The congregations must have a structure that permits them to develop and to meet the needs of the people, rather than being a branch office for the denominational bureaucracy.

Laypeople often speak positively of their church as being a family. They value the warm fellowship they experience in the congregation. Church structure should reinforce these characteristics. Instead, we have developed a complex organization that is more suitable to running a highly centralized business than to forming a family—a white collar corporate model of organization. This is designed to maintain the institution and to provide local outlets for the programs of the general agencies, as if power flowed from the top down. In the church, power rightly flows from the bottom up—up from strong congregations.

Structure is never changed easily because too many powerful people and groups have a vested interest in the *status quo*. A vital denomination, however, must have vital congregations. These require an organization that gives the local churches both the freedom and the responsibility to develop their ministry and program. Structure can produce liberation or stagnation. United Methodism needs to move to one that provides the liberation for a vital witness and ministry by each local church.

Notes

1. *Doctrines and Disciplines of The Methodist Church 1940* (New York: The Methodist Publishing House, 1940), par. 528–534.

2. *Doctrines and Disciplines of The Methodist Church 1952* (Nashville: The Methodist Publishing House, 1952), par. 219.

3. Richard B. Wilke, *And Are We Yet Alive* (Nashville: Abingdon Press, 1986), p. 29.

Trust the Laity

Chapter 9. The Wesleyan revival in eighteenth-century England was in great part John Wesley's inspired attempt to reform the established Church of England through a reformation of the laity. Wesley knew enough about the theological and practical implications of the doctrine of the church to know that the laity are the church. Any revitalization of the church must proceed from the bottom up. Wesley knew enough about church history to know that any time the church becomes dominated by the self-interest and aspirations of the clergy, the church declines. Although John Wesley was a superbly educated person, a beneficiary of the best classical education Oxford had to offer, his true genius lay in his ability to speak to the laypeople in ways that could be understood and appropriated in everyday life. Wesley's use of lay preachers, the prominent role of women in early Methodist societies, and the mutual discipline all the laity shared within the life of the "classes" are some of the examples of the ways in which Wesley helped to return the church to the laity.

Wesley's scriptural warrant was the Protestant doctrine of the "priesthood of believers"—the belief that each Christian is "ordained" by virtue of his or her baptism to be a priest to his or her neighbor. The First Epistle of Peter addresses all the church, not just the clergy, when it says to newly baptized Christians:

You are a chosen race, a royal priesthood, a holy nation, God's own people, that you may declare the wonderful deeds of him who called you out of darkness into his marvelous light. Once you were no people but now you are God's people; once you had not received mercy but now you have received mercy. (I Peter 2:9-10)

All Christians, by our baptism, are commissioned to evangelize, to witness, to teach, to heal, and to proclaim the Word of God to one another and to the world. The church exists to provide laity with the equipment they need to fulfill their baptismal commission, to enable us to receive the strengths, wisdom, skills, and insights we need to be faithful as a visible witness to the lordship of Christ.

Whose Church?

Despite Wesley's desire to return the church to the laity, our present structure, as well as some of our history, mitigate against his good intentions. In the beginning, Wesley had no intention of founding new congregations. He sought to use his lay preachers as a means of revitalizing the parishes of the Church of England through vigorous preaching and the tight, closely knit organization of his class meetings. Wesley organized his lay preachers into conferences, which he presided over at annual meetings to give them directions for their duties for the next year.

When Methodism eventually developed into a new church, first in America and then in England, this annual conference of preachers continued to be a basic organizational structure of Methodism. In other words, Methodism was a new denomination, organized, led, and even dominated by its clergy. This enabled our church to mobilize rapidly and to deploy its clergy on the farthest reaches of the American frontier. The organization of the Methodist Episcopal Church, centered on a highly disciplined and dedicated group of circuit riders, was well suited to the demands of the new frontier. The church grew rapidly; yet, it was a church that had no room for lay guidance and input beyond the local church level. Bishops appointed the traveling preachers to various congregations without lay consultation.

While resulting in efficient deployment and frontier evangelism, this domination of the church by the clergy has caused problems throughout the history of American Methodism. It was a source of a major division among Methodists in 1830. Over the years, the Methodist Church and the Evangelical United Brethren Church took various steps to include the laity within the upper echelons of the denomination's organization. Even though our laity are prohibited from voting on ministerial matters, beyond the Pastor-Staff Relations Committee's approval of candidates for ordination, laity now enjoy equal representation at the annual jurisdictional and general conference levels.

Unfortunately, equal representation and an equal number of votes does not ensure that the laity are equally influential as clergy in the governance of The United Methodist Church. We are still a church in which the clergy give most of the leadership and determine most of the policies. Of course, some of this is quite natural. The laity have a right to expect that their clergy are people who are called by God for the task of leadership within the church. Laity expect their clergy to be particularly knowledgeable about the history, the theology, and the organization of the church. Earlier, in chapter 5 of this book, it was argued that the church must have leaders instead of managers. But real leaders never forget that their position is a trust they exercise as stewards for the benefit of all the church's members.

Over a decade and a half ago, Jeffery Hadden wrote a book entitled *The Gathering Storm in the Churches,* in which he argued that a storm was brewing because of the growing gap between the opinions and direction of Protestant clergy when compared to Protestant laity. He states that the clergy had developed a new understanding of the meaning and implications of the Christian faith but, "have not succeeded in communicating this understanding to laity."[1] This difference was a sign of troubled times to come. We do not believe that Hadden's predicted storm has occurred in United Methodism. The laity have docilely stood by, not seriously challenging the clergy, while the church has declined. Laypeople have been expected to be loyal, to voice their opinions in church debates, and to pay the bills, but were told that they must accept without question the appointment, promotion, and deployment of the clergy.

A Guild Mentality

The gap between laity and the clergy was widened with the increased educational requirements for ordination. Over the years, seminary education has become a requirement for virtually all United Methodist clergy. It should be noted that the pressure to increase the educational requirements of clergy has come from the ministers, not from the laity. Thus our clergy have followed many other professions in increasing the complexity and the requirements for certification to practice in the profession. While the pressure to increase the educational requirements for clergy has many desirable consequences, it is also a means of our clergy's assuring themselves that the ministry is a "profession," similar to medicine or law. This implies that the clergy possess special esoteric skills, unusual acquired insights, or other attributes by virtue of their seminary education, ordination, and admission into the annual conference, apart from their function as servants of the church.

The result is a mentality that tends to ensure that only those persons who will fit into the system are encouraged and finally admitted. Students early in their seminary careers discover what the denomination expects of them and adapt to the system. They quickly learn how to be loyal organizationalists. We should all worry that creative and innovative leadership, which the denomination needs, is not likely to come from men and women who have so quickly subscribed to the institutional status quo.

The trend has been for the clergy to bring more persons like themselves into the guild and to exclude other types of pastors. For many years, the local preacher (later known as approved supply pastor, lay pastor, and now local pastor) played a significant role in Methodism. The number of lay pastors has decreased, and the goal seems to be to phase them out altogether. In 1972, the category associate member of the annual conference was created. This enables certain local pastors, for all practical purposes, to be full members of an annual conference. They are excluded from voting on constitutional amendments, delegates to the general and jurisdictional conferences, and matters of ordination, character, and conference relations of ministers. The expectation is that the local pastors will move toward associate or full membership in the annual conference. The *Discipline* provides that full-time local pastors must complete the educational requirements within eight years and part-time persons within ten years, although a provision for annual extensions is made. Many local pastors feel under considerable pressure to become associate members if they are to be permitted to continue in the ministry.

A guild expects its members to be homogeneous. This is already causing problems in The United Methodist Church. First, it is more difficult for churches of small membership to secure the services of part-time clergy. As an increasingly high proportion of ministers are either full or associate conference members, they will have to be given full-time appointments. The church that is not geographically located so that it can become part of a circuit and is too small to employ a full-time minister can be in serious difficulty. The proportion of United Methodist expenditures needed to support the clergy has been slowly increasing. In 1970, the church spent 28 percent of all money on ministerial support; in 1984 the proportion was 32 percent.

The pressure to have all clergy seminary trained and full members of an annual conference is increasing the difficulty of securing pastors for our ethnic congregations. The denomination has not been successful in its attempt to recruit an adequate number of ethnic ministerial candidates, despite the availability of scholarship assistance. One conference leader lamented, "We need more large black congregations. You can't expect the well-trained seminary graduate to want to serve the small black churches we have in this district." This person was correct. Some seminary graduates, both black and white, resist serving certain types of congregations. This fact, combined with the shortage of ethnic pastors, has created a serious problem.

The only way The United Methodist Church is going to provide ministerial leadership for many small black, Hispanic, and other ethnic congregations is to utilize more full and part-time local pastors. This would also allow indigenous leaders from the ethnic communities to emerge.

Three or four years of seminary education appear not only to make our clergy more sophisticated intellectually, but also to remove them from the cultural and social level of many people who most need the church. Some of the prospects for evangelization are the unchurched who live in government subsidized housing developments, new immigrant communities and even some rural communities. But our newly professionalized clergy may be ill-equipped or too socially aloof to work with these persons. The training of and reliance on indigenous part-time local pastors (in much the same fashion as their use by Wesley) could be the single most significant step we could take toward winning millions of new United Methodists.

Ministry as Vocation

We believe that the ordained ministry is best described not as a profession, but as a *vocation*. The church (the laity) is the instrument of God in calling certain baptized Christians to bear the special burden of ordination. Ordination derives its meaning not from the special skills an ordained minister may acquire in seminary, but rather from that person's being set apart by the church for work the church needs done.

The roots of the ordained ministry are hinted at in the New Testament. Jesus tells his disciples, "It shall not be so [as it is among worldly leaders] among you" (Mark 10:43). The clergy, unlike some of the world's other leaders and professionals, are not to lead our people by "domineering over those in your charge but being examples to the flock" (I Peter 5:3).

After having attended a seminary, too many of our clergy

feel that the laypeople do not really understand the Christian faith, even though it is the laity who give meaning and purpose to the pastoral ministry in the first place. Apart from service in equipping and upbuilding the laity, clergy have no real function in the church. The purpose of all our preaching, visiting, teaching, evangelization, and healing ministries is the equipment of the "priests." Yet many ministers feel that there is a gap between what they have learned in seminary and what the laity believe. The pastor is uncomfortable with what goes on in the adult Bible study class. In fact, there is a feeling among the ministers that those who have not had the advantage of a seminary education can't really understand the faith. Perhaps that is a reason United Methodism provides so much local church organization. It keeps the lay members busy with internal, institutional chores, rather than releasing them to be about their ministry in the world.

A deep and empowering faith does not result from higher education. Education may enhance understanding and deepen faith, but most clergy must admit that the springs of faith lie in one's experience of the presence of Christ within the church, not from the ability to use the historical critical method with scripture or to apply theological jargon. Renewal requires that laypeople wrestle with the theological issues. The clergy must trust the laypeople to witness to their experience of the grace of God, not simply to serve on the finance committee.

One reason our recent debates over who should be ordained (e.g., to ordain or not to ordain homosexuals) have been especially bitter is that the laity know, in our church, they have no real voice in the appointment process. There is an increasing feeling that the conference leaders are taking care of the clergy at the expense of the churches. Francis Asbury's autocratic style in deploying his traveling preachers may have been an effective system in the early nineteenth century, but one may question whether such methods are appropriate two centuries later. We need to trust the laypeople to have the best interests of their church at heart.

The Pastor-Staff Relations Committee of one church of

our acquaintance went through a long process of evaluating the programs and ministry of their church along with their pastor's leadership. They, and their pastor, came to the mutual conclusion that it would probably be best for the future of the congregation if the pastor were moved that year. After all, the pastor had already been at that church for five years and all agreed that a change would be beneficial. Here was an opportunity for our appointment system to function at its best—in helping a church to go through the potentially difficult process of a change in pastoral leadership.

The bishop and the cabinet, after considering the committee's request, told them that, "There are no suitable appointments for this pastor this year. Keep him another year and we shall move him when more suitable appointments become available." The committee regretted that the church had to wait another year, but in view of the pastor's faithful past service, they agreed to wait. The next year, they went through the same process and came to the same conclusion: It would be best for their pastor and the congregation for him to be moved. This time, more negative comments came out about the pastor's leadership. Some in the church did not like the pastor's stand on various social and political issues. They made threats that if the pastor were not moved this time, they would move to another church. Their threats were taken by the bishop as an attack on "the system." In order to flex his muscle, the bishop wrote a long letter to the church and directed that the letter should be read from the pulpit by the Chairperson of the Pastor-Staff Relations Committee. The letter stated that it was the bishop's prerogative to appoint ministers to churches, and he had decided that, "Due to the pastor's courageous social witness," he was determined to have the pastor stay another year and resist the efforts of those who opposed him.

The result of all of this was that a large number of members of the church moved to other congregations, not all of them United Methodist. A clergy-dominated appointment system remained in place, but at great expense to this particular congregation.

"Doesn't the bishop know that the Middle Ages have

ended?" asked the Chairperson of the Pastor-Staff Relations Committee. We believe the day is quickly coming to a close when our laity will accept the premise that "Father knows best," particularly when they have often seen the clerical muscle flexed, not out of great concern for the best interest of individual congregations, but for the self-interest of the clergy.

American churches exist in a consumer society. People are demanding and getting a part in decisions affecting their lives. A generation ago, our church could count on our people to be generally loyal to the system, to stick with the system, even when the system did not appear immediately to benefit their personal needs or the needs of their congregation. The increased feeling among laity that the church does not really have their interests at heart is contributing to the growing number of people who feel little loyalty to the denomination per se. If our denomination is unresponsive and closed to the voice of the laity, people will go elsewhere.

Listen to the Laity

After a most painful period of unemployment, plant closings, and the loss of once lucrative markets to better managed companies, American businesses seem at last to be learning an important principle: Listen to the customer! American consumers have told American automobile producers, for instance, that they want quality and that they are willing to pay for it. Those companies that have listened to the customers and have responded are regaining lost markets. Those companies that doggedly went on producing as they always had, despite consumer complaints, are going out of business. Of course, the laity are much more than "customers." As we have said elsewhere in this book, the local congregation is much more significant than a mere branch office for the national church's programs and crusades. The church is greater than even the clergy or the laity. The laity do not always know the best course for the church, nor do they claim to.

But our laity are worth listening to. They are the Christians who must live the faith within the factories, schools, nursing homes, and offices. In the 1960s and 1970s, when the professional educators who were in charge of our church school curriculum resources decided to produce Sunday school literature that would bring more "respectable theology" to the lowly laity, the laypeople responded by going to non-United Methodist publishing houses for their literature. They complained that many of the people could not read or understand or teach the curricula that their church was busy producing. When the United Methodist Publishing House made earnest attempts to listen to the laity and to ask them what type of resources they needed in their Christian education class rooms, it responded by producing what the "customers" asked for, and sales of official United Methodist curricula increased. Unfortunately, not all church leaders and agencies saw the point, and so they still perceive the laity as troops to be ordered about, instead of as potential customers to be won.

Many laity say that they do not wish to see the biblical names of God changed in worship and educational materials in the interest of allegedly "inclusive language." The response of some of the clergy? "The laity need to have their consciousness raised about this issue." In other words, the laity are ignorant and need to be taught, or else legislatively coerced, through the *Discipline* into our clericalized opinions. If a clerical elite attempts to dominate the church and arrogantly attempts to force its opinions and programs on the laity, there will be a backlash. This may take the form of dropping out of the church or a reactionary uprising, and possibly some of both.

As highlighted earlier, the clergy have a responsibility to teach in the congregation. However, Christian teachers begin with the assumption that the church belongs to all Christians, particularly to those Christians who must live out the faith in their daily life and work in the world, so the opinions of these Christians must be taken seriously. Down through the ages, there has tended to be little limit to the arrogant assumption, lurking within every church, that the church exists for the clergy.

We deplore how the meetings of our annual and general conferences have become more consumed with ministerial matters—debates over pensions, appointments, and qualifications of clergy. We note how local church expenditures for clergy pensions, for minimum salary funds, and for ministerial education have risen at a geometric rate in the last decade, consuming an ever larger share of the church's budget. All of this is disturbing evidence of the growing clericalization of our church.

The laity must again "own" the church. In our system, clergy are members, not of local churches, but of their annual conference. Therefore, there is a tendency for the clergy to feel that their future lies, and that their ministry will be evaluated, not by their service to the local congregation, but by their loyalty to and compatibility with the annual conference. Many are tempted to view the local congregation as a stepping stone to a better appointment, a temporary way station on the way up the conference ladder. Chapter 11 notes the potentially debilitating effect this mentality has on preaching within our church. It affects many other areas of life within the local church as well.

We believe that our system is basically sound, for there is much to be said for a system of clergy deployment that has a reasonable degree of independence and a vision beyond the concerns of the local church—*if the laity also do their part in voicing the concerns and insights of their local congregation.* The laity must remind themselves that this is "their" church. They will be here in this community and in this church long after the pastor has moved elsewhere. They will be able to see the opportunities for mission within their own community, which the pastor, as a relative newcomer to the community, may miss. They know the history, the traditions, and the style of their congregation. They must assert that tradition, instruct their new pastor in their past, or else be what too many of our United Methodist Churches have become—bland, unexciting, undistinguishable clones of one another.

In the past few years, we have talked much of "pluralism" in our church. The term may be useful in signifying our inability to appeal to any common authority to settle our theological fragmentation, but the term is only an empty slogan when it comes to the official attitude about local churches. A plurality of differences among congregations is a threat to the clergy. The clergy have a stake in generalizing their congregations, in making every United Methodist congregation look much like every other, in suppressing differences and distinctive characteristics, in ousting maverick members, and in fostering as much uniformity as possible. Clergy do this because it is easier for our clergy to serve such congregations. Uniformity among congregations requires less adaptation among the clergy who serve them. Uniformity also requires less creativity among the clergy who appoint other clergy. It is easier for bishops and district superintendents to move clergy around among such churches. Our system does not tolerate much deviation from the norm, be it conservative or liberal. Yet, the future belongs to those congregations who know who they are and who assert that identity with boldness. In a town in which every United Methodist church looks like every other United Methodist church, all will lose. Lacking choice, theological alternatives, and differences in style of worship, we shall all decline into a dull shade of gray. This attitude has been a disaster in our meager attempts to reach the ethnic populations and has been a factor in our inability to attract new members within a competitive, voluntaristic American church environment, in which people select churches on the basis of their assessment of that church's ability to meet their needs.

All United Methodists should anticipate the day when the laity will rise up and say to their appointed clergy, "We welcome you here to our congregation and look forward to your leadership among us. But realizing that you will be with us for only a while, we will tell you the story of our church. We will identify for you the aspects of this church that make us love it, the crises we have endured, and our dreams for the future. We will listen to your dreams and your insights about how we might be more faithful, but first you must respect what God has done here among us."

The United Methodist system functions best as a creative balance between an ordained ministry that upholds certain values and commitments and boldly represents them, in word and deed, before the churches to which they are sent and a committed laity that articulates and enacts the gospel within thousands of localities across our nation. A revitalized United Methodist Church requires that we trust the laity to perform their unique ministry and that the laity trust themselves to minister.

Note

1. Jeffrey K. Hadden, *The Gathering Storm in the Churches* (Garden City, N. Y.: Doubleday, 1969), p. 230.

Give Priority to Sunday Morning

Chapter 10. Some time ago, Leander Keck, who later became the dean of the Yale Divinity School, charged that many of our pastors have allowed "sundry matters to displace Sunday matters." Watching many of us pastors at work, the laity might conclude that we are more heavily invested in any other pastoral duty than the one the laity consistently rate as the most important—preaching and leadership of worship. In a church in which one of the authors formerly served as pastor, the Pastor-Staff Relations Committee was asked to help their new pastor decide which pastoral duties were most important for the life of that congregation. The pastor listed each of his pastoral activities on a notecard, everything from visiting the sick to composing each week's worship bulletin. Then the pastor shuffled the cards and gave them to the committee, asking the committee to sort them according to their priority for this congregation. When he returned to the room, he was surprised that they listed preaching as the most important activity, followed by visitation of seriously ill members, the planning and leadership of worship, visitation of prospective members, and so on. The pastor was surprised, since that congregation had experienced a steady decline in membership over the past decade. He thought that visitation of prospective members might be at the top of their list.

"If you preach sermons that really relate to people's lives, if the Sunday service is exciting and important, we will bring the new members here," said one of the laypersons.

This response has been confirmed by observation of growing congregations across the country. Last year, when Bishop Richard B. Wilke convened the pastors of a variety of growing churches, they agreed that, among all the factors contributing to the growth or decline of a church, preaching and Sunday morning worship are primary.

When a family moves to a new town and begins to look for a church, their first encounter with a church will, in the great majority of cases, be the Sunday morning worship service. If they like what they see and hear, if something seems to be happening there, they may return next week to visit the church school or other smaller group. Their pattern of encounter with the church has biblical and historical precedent. Church or Sunday schools, small support groups, gymnasiums, publishing houses, even the clergy themselves, all are secondary inventions of the church. All are subsequent developments to the primary and basic experience of Christians coming together to worship God. A church or a pastor who allows other matters to crowd out Sunday matters is in grave danger of losing the main mark and the primary reason for the existence of the church. If it doesn't happen here, on Sunday, for the church, it doesn't happen anywhere.

There is cause for concern because the data on Sunday morning worship signal that we have reached a crisis in the participation of our people in the main gathering and sending event of the church. With 9,266,853 members in 1984, the average worship attendance was 3,549,347 persons. In other words, when the church gathers for worship, the average attendance is equal to only 38 percent of our members. Perhaps more disturbing is the overall trend in attendance. In the past fourteen years, our average worship attendance has decreased 11 percent. In sheer numbers, 442,530 fewer persons were present for Sunday morning worship in United Methodist Churches in 1984 than in 1971.

The numbers would be disturbing for any church, but they are particularly disheartening for United Methodists. We heirs of Wesley have not been known for the depth of our theology. We are a church that was born amid Wesley's quest for an experiential faith, the religion of the warm heart. In small prayer groups, in singing the rousing hymns of the Wesleys, in frontier revivals, Methodists and EUBs experienced the Wesleyan truth that religion, while not only of the heart, is primarily an encounter, an experience of the risen Christ within our gatherings for worship. When United Methodists lose the Sunday service as the main focus of our life together, we have lost the very source of our life; we have become severed from the wellspring of our distinctive witness.

The Wesleyan revival was, in part, a liturgical revival. It wedded many of the services and forms of the Anglican *Book of Common Prayer* with a straightforward, enthusiastic call to new life in Christ within the Body of Christ. Wesley frequently wrote about the centrality of the sacraments for sustaining the Christian life. Charles Wesley transformed the worship of the church universal through thousands of his hymns. John Wesley stressed the centrality of preaching, urging his traveling preachers to study and to inculcate not only the Bible, but also his sermons. Without a vital sacramental life, without inspiring, singable, lively hymns and engaging, biblical, and applicable sermons, United Methodists have very little left on Sunday except to become victims of dry, tedious, petty moralism or to be enlisted in the latest crusades of the political left or right. Alas, in many of our congregations, this is the present state of affairs.

Earlier it was noted that there is a great need in our time for Christian formation, the careful, long-term, intentional formation of Christians who are able to articulate and to live their faith in daily life. "To spread scriptural holiness throughout the land" was the way the early American Methodists expressed it. In every region of United Methodism, laity, time and again, assert that they want a pastor who is a "spiritual leader." While many may disagree about the specific qualities present in such a leader, there is agreement that this person should be someone who is concerned about sacred things, able to talk about the experience of the holy, someone who personally knows God and is able to be helpful to others in their spiritual journey. The laity seem to have learned, perhaps before some of our pastors, that the living of the Christian life is too difficult without spiritual formation.

Spiritual formation occurs in many ways in the congregation's life together, but in no more important way, to no larger numbers of the congregation, than on Sunday morning. Here is where the average member is confronted by the claims of the gospel. Here is where the story of Christ and his church is told, reiterated, and internalized. It is little wonder then that, every time during the church's history when questions of Christian identity were raised, reformers eventually had to become reformers of worship. Sunday morning—at the Lord's table, at the baptismal font, and at the pulpit—is the primary place where Christians have always discovered and recovered who they are and whose they are.

Sunday Morning Problems

When consideration is given to the ways of revitalizing the Sunday morning service, the contemporary heirs of John Wesley are faced with some very real problems, one of which is preaching. One central activity of the early Methodist revival was preaching, as evidenced by the thousands of sermons Wesley preached. It is still primary in the contemporary church. The current *Discipline* lists twelve tasks of the minister. The first is, "To preach the Word, read and teach the Scriptures, and engage the people in study and witness" (par. 439.1).

Wesley published his sermons to provide doctrinal guidance to his followers, issuing four volumes in a fourteen-year period. Today, preaching and the content of sermons continues to involve questions about orthodox doctrine, biblical interpretation, ethical issues, and the whole complex of factors that make up vital Christian proclamation. Whenever the church debates the qualities of "good preaching," there will be disagreements about what constitutes "good sermons." But there should be no disagreement that preaching is a primary activity of our pastors.

Too many United Methodist laity express bafflement that their pastors allow almost any other pastoral activity to distract their attention from the task of preparing and delivering sermons. At best, laity will sometimes comment, "Well, our pastor isn't much of a preacher, but he is a very loving pastor"—a dubious compliment. Imagine someone saying, "She is a wonderful physician; she just can't stand to be around people," or "He is a great mechanic; he just refuses to get his hands dirty fixing a car." At other times, laity will express their displeasure with the current state of preaching through outright criticisms, saying that sermons are dull and boring; sermons are read as if they were academic lectures, rather than Christian proclamation; sermons are political or psychological, rather than biblical; or preachers are obviously unprepared or obviously ill at ease while preaching. Some laity presume that their preacher has spent most of his or her week preparing for the sermon and are thus particularly confused when the pastor is so embarrassingly unprepared to lead in the main public activity of the clergy.

We believe that the problem with preaching is not primarily a lack of sincerity or commitment on the part of the preachers. There are significant structural and institutional reasons why "sundry matters have displaced Sunday matters" in our church. For one thing, there are few "rewards" for good preaching. In many denominations, a pastor is selected by a congregation only after an interview and a trial sermon or after some committee—very often called the pulpit committee—in the congregation has had the opportunity to listen to and to evaluate that pastor's preaching in his or her present church. But our pastors are evaluated and appointed by other clergy who probably have never heard them preach. A district superintendent may go on hearsay, perhaps conducting an informal poll of a few Pastor-Parish Relations Committee members, asking them, "How do you like George as a preacher?" But there is generally no systematic attempt on the part of the bishop or district superintendent to learn how well a pastor is invested in his or her preaching. Unless laity complain, and do so vehemently, it is assumed that the individual's preaching is satisfactory.

A person who is newly ordained quickly learns that advancement in the United Methodist system is not predicated upon good preaching. He or she can look around at the persons who are in prestigious churches in the conference or persons who are serving on conference boards and agencies and quickly surmise that they are appointed or elected for reasons other than their ability to preach. Too often, when our bishops preach, they do not provide good models for the rest of the clergy. Their preaching preparation has fallen victim to the excessive demands of administration, attendance at national meetings, and other bureaucratic responsibilities. A seminary professor once told his class to be sure to hear the newly elected bishop preach in the chapel one morning, commenting, "He hasn't been a bishop long enough to have lost his ability to preach." If the bishop does not have time to prepare for preaching, why should a local church pastor be expected to prepare?

Good preaching takes time, talent, and a lifetime of work. Though our laity may say that they want good preaching, they may have little idea of how much time, energy, and commitment good preaching takes. The preparation of sermons is a lonely, private enterprise. No one sees the hours a pastor may devote to a twenty-minute sermon. No wonder then that many pastors devote themselves to more visible activities—visiting at the hospital, administering the church, working with the youth. Some sermons are well prepared and thoughtfully delivered, yet, fail to "work" for some reason. The Word is proclaimed not only by the preacher's hard work, but also by the power of the Holy Spirit, which empowers both the sermon and the ability of the congregation to hear. Because good preaching is so difficult to achieve and to predict, many of our clergy are tempted toward more predictable, more achievable, more measurable pastoral activities.

Certainly, great preaching is an art, a matter of talent as well as hard work. But good preaching is not some mystical gift. Preaching is ultimately a skill that can be learned like any other skill. Some clergy may already have gifts and graces that equip them to be good preachers. Others may have to substitute hard work and disciplined training for their lack of talent. But preaching can be improved if we think that it is important to have good preaching and if we give our pastors the tools and the time they need to preach. Laity need to be told what it takes for a preacher to preach well—time for quiet meditation and study, an ongoing program of continuing education, periodic opportunities for rest and spiritual renewal. We believe that the laity will be willing to provide the resources and the support their pastors need to develop their preaching skills, for our laity are the strongest advocates of the need for pastors who are spiritual guides and good preachers—if they can be shown that their resources and support are used to good advantage.

Sunday Morning Possibilities

Fortunately, United Methodism can benefit from the current revival of interest in Christian preaching and the current renewal of Christian worship. Across all denominational lines, many Christian congregations are rediscovering the joy of vibrant, biblically based worship. The Roman Catholic Church, which once downplayed preaching, has rediscovered the balance of Word and Table, which we Protestants (in theory at least) stressed. We Protestants, after decades of neglect of the sacraments (a particularly strange state of affairs for United Methodists, considering Wesley's own views of the centrality of the sacraments) are learning again the power of the historic symbols and dramatic actions in Christian worship.

But we cannot benefit from these movements unless United Methodists recover the centrality of Sunday in the life of our congregations. Those who appoint our clergy, our bishops, and our district superintendents must themselves be models of commitment to vibrant preaching and worship, and they must find ways to evaluate the Sunday morning leadership of the clergy under their care. No business would think of hiring someone to manage some aspect of their business without first inquiring into that person's possession of the necessary skills to do the job; yet, we do it all the time!

Few laity would understand, nor should they, how someone who has not had to study and practice preaching and worship can be appointed to serve a church. For all practical purposes, we require a seminary education for our clergy; yet, some seminaries still do not have full-time professors of Christian worship. It is still possible to be ordained in some annual conferences without having either adequate training or demonstrated ability in preaching. Preaching and worship leadership are primary skills for our clergy and are skills that can be learned. If someone, for some physical or emotional reason, does not have the ability to learn these skills, that person should be counseled to seek some means of service in the church other than the parish ministry. The Sunday worship of the congregation is simply too important to allow anyone, for whatever reason, to disrupt or to deny our people the weekly privilege of hearing and enacting God's presence in Word and sacrament.

It is encouraging to see the development of new, biblically based, ecumenically received, historically and theologically sound worship services for use in our church, now found in *The Book of Services* and (in Spanish) *Cultus Principales*.[1] Still, an embarrassingly large number of our congregations have never even seen the "new" services of the Lord's Supper (1972) and Christian baptism (1979), mainly because their pastors have not taken the time and the initiative to introduce these new resources. A great step toward revitalized, engaging, full services on Sunday morning would be for pastors to devote their efforts to introducing these services to their congregations.

A warning about this matter of liturgical innovation must be given. One reason the Wesleys encountered a lethargic Church of England, in which great numbers of the English people had withdrawn from Sunday services and in which the sacraments were infrequently celebrated, was that, two centuries before the Wesleys, liturgical change had been shoved down the throats of the English people by royal edict. The people did what they have always done when they have been the victims of thoughtless, high-handed, and poorly interpreted changes in worship—they simply withdrew from

Sunday worship. When a new hymnal, a new order of worship, or a new style of preaching is introduced into a congregation, it must be done with the utmost patience, interpretation, and most important of all, lay consultation and leadership, knowing that worship is the central activity of the church. If our new *Book of Hymns* is poorly introduced into the local church, United Methodists could lose our single, central instrument of liturgical unity, and the results will have devastating consequences. Our people often become angry and resentful when their pastors force them into areas of innovation without first carefully preparing them for the innovation and soliciting their reaction. United Methodism has wisely been rather congregationalist in its approach to worship. Worship orders and forms are carefully devised for our congregations, and our pastors and congregations are encouraged to use these services. But use of our services is still a matter of local option—and should always remain a local option—dependent on the pastor and the congregation's own adaptation of the services and assessment of their congregational situation. The congregation, including its socio-economic situation, its accustomed style and its composition, is an important factor to consider in ordering our worship. This applies not only to the introduction of new services, but also to the retention of old ones.

For every congregation that is fearful of liturgical innovation, more congregations are probably bored with their present orders of worship. These congregations are worshiping the way they do on Sunday morning, not because it is a valued part of their life together, but simply because this is the way their current pastor has decreed that they will worship. More than likely, the current pastor is merely doing what he or she has done at the last five charges he or she has served, rather than really taking the congregation's needs, their reactions to the present style of worship, or our denomination's new worship service options into account. If every pastor would dare to ask the laity what they think about his or her preaching and about the current order, style, and content of public worship in the church, that would be a marvelous (though possibly painful for the pastor) way to begin to recover the centrality and vitality of Sunday morning.

The first *Discipline* published in America set standards that are valid today. In answer to the question, "What is the duty of a preacher?" the first listed was, "To preach."[2] The directions for public worship were:

> Let the morning-service consist of singing, prayer, the reading of a chapter out of the Old Testament, and another out of the New, and preaching. . . .
> A peculiar blessing accompanies the public reading as well as preaching the word of God to attentive, believing souls. And in these days of infidelity, nothing should be omitted, which may lead the people to the love of the holy bible.[3]

Notes

1. *The Book of Services* (Nashville: The United Methodist Publishing House, 1985).

2. Frederick A. Norwood, ed. *Doctrines and Discipline of the Methodist Episcopal Church in America,* facsimile edition (Rutland, Vt.: Academy Books, 1979), p. 58.

3. *Ibid.,* pp. 120-21.

To Serve the Present Age

Chapter 11. A book on strategies to revitalize The United Methodist Church is nothing more than an interesting academic exercise, unless something happens as a result. People must take specific actions if our church is to reverse the downward spiral of the past two decades and increase the effectiveness of its witness and ministry. We are optimistic that our church already has the structure and the people to revitalize United Methodism. This concludng chapter will present some next steps: what should be done and by whom. These steps do not encompass everything that must be done, but they are a beginning. We believe that they are the most important steps to be taken.

Radical changes in the structure of the denomination are not necessary. Superficial tinkering with the ecclesiastical machinery would only divert time and energy from more important tasks. Instead, radical changes in the way we operate as a denomination are absolutely essential. Our problem is not that we need new forms of organization, but that *we are not using our present structure in ways that will create a vital and growing church.* Our system is being misused for the benefit of certain groups, rather than to further the purpose of the entire church. All United Methodists—the laity, the clergy, and the denominational leaders—bear responsibility for helping make the changes necessary for the revitalization of the church. There are some tasks that fall to all United

Methodists; others are the primary responsibility of the laity, the clergy, or certain denominational leaders. Below is a proposed agenda for the revitalization of United Methodism.

For All United Methodist People

Affirming the Wesleyan heritage is the responsibility of every United Methodist. A vital church must know who it is, what it believes, and why it operates as it does. We are not advocating a form of denominational triumphalism, but a knowledge and an appreciation of our distinctive identity. The United Methodist Church is not a bland, unexciting shade of gray; we really do have something special to offer people—a unique experience and expression of the Christian faith. Every local church must give attention to this matter.

Local churches need more courses in historic United Methodism and the Wesleyan spirit. This is important for all church members, because it cannot be assumed that even people who have grown up in our church have an adequate knowledge of their heritage. It is critical for persons who are received by transfer from other denominations to learn about United Methodism. We must respect our heritage enough to insist that new members submit to instruction. The person who recently commented, "I like being a Methodist because you can believe anything you want to," typifies the problem. A wide range of programs, from Sunday school classes to special events, can be designed to help people understand and appreciate their church. An increasing number of materials is already available; more will be needed, particularly those that utilize new video possibilities.

Discovering the real purpose of the church is also a matter to which all United Methodists must give attention. Our church is fragmented. We have become involved in so many programs, have formed so many alliances with a variety of religious and secular groups, and have championed so many contradictory causes that we no longer know what is our unique task. To recover the real purpose of the church will not be easy because many of the activities in which we have been involved are socially useful, if not necessarily Christian, and all have their champions within our bureaucracy.

Each congregation needs to ask itself the questions: "Who are we?" and "What are we trying to accomplish?" To begin to answer these questions requires a determination of the criteria by which a particular activity is judged to have an appropriate claim on the church's limited resources. Each local church should prepare a statement of mission, utilizing the statements on the mission of the church in the *Discipline,* by which its program could be measured. The budget could then be studied to see if expenditures are in line with the congregation's purpose.

The development of a statement of local mission or purpose will require much soul searching. It will force people to take account of their understanding of the faith, their heritage, and the situation in which their church exists today. The completion of this task would enable the members to better understand their faith and the way that faith is lived out through the local Christian community. It would give focus to the congregation's work and enable the people to concentrate their efforts on activities and goals that are consistent with their understanding of their purpose.

For the Laity

Methodism has, from its earliest days, been a church in which the clergy have been dominant. The last half century has seen the inclusion of increasing numbers of laypersons in official voting positions until they now constitute one half of the members of many church bodies, including the General Conference, the Jurisdictional Conferences, and the Annual Conferences. Nevertheless many lay officials follow the leadership of the clergy, who continue to be the dominant force in the denomination.

United Methodist laypersons, even after two hundred years, tend to be too passive. The laity expect—as they have a right to expect—competent and dedicated leadership from the clergy. In those cases in which such leadership is not forthcoming, they tolerate the individual, hoping for a change in the near future. Because they are loyal church members and do not want to cause trouble, many laypeople are reluctant to challenge the clergy or the system. Furthermore, there is the widespread belief that a congregation that is uncooperative, that gives its minister a hard time, or that doesn't pay its apportionments will be "punished" by the clerical guild by being given a less competent pastor. Some district superintendents encourage this belief, and there are enough examples to give it credibility.

Lay members can and must do several things if the church is to experience revitalization. They must be more assertive, even if their assertiveness results in conflict. They must be less accepting of poor performance of the clergy. If a minister is preaching poorly, reusing old sermons, or neglecting the sacraments, the laypeople should let him or her know that the congregation expects and deserves more competent leadership. This would be better than complaining to one another and attending church less frequently.

Passivity on the part of the laity is bad for all. It is bad for the pastor because it permits a less than satisfactory performance to continue. It is bad for the lay members because they are not adequately served. It is bad for the congregation because it results in bad situations being allowed to continue and decreases the church's overall effectiveness.

An effective denomination depends on vital local churches. The denominational outreach and benevolent programs represent an extension of the ministry of the local churches and are possible only because of the financial support United Methodists provide. The energy and the commitment that are gathered in local churches are the foundation for everything else done by the denomination. First priority must be given to strengthening the local church and to making it more effective. A good rule to follow is: Any clergy appointment system, method of organization, or church program that debilitates the life of the local church is bad for the whole church.

The laity will have to assume responsibility for making the local church the major priority. The clergy are members of the annual conference and perceive their career as dependent on their loyalty to the larger organization, rather than to their performance in the local church. What we are asking for is a drastic departure from the role laity have played in the church. A more assertive laity will not be received enthusiastically by many of the clergy and church bureaucrats. While there has been an attempt to involve more laity, it has been in ways that ensure that they would not threaten the institutional status quo. What is needed is a more assertive laity, who will exert real influence on the course of the church.

The laity must be more assertive and insist that their local church respond effectively to the needs of the members and of the community. It is the laity who must insist that the local church receive first priority. Given the nature of United Methodism, it is unlikely that the laity will have any significant effect on the denominational organization or on the boards and agencies. However, a more assertive laity could ensure that the church structure would not become an undue burden or a handicap to the local congregation. The faithful congregation will be here, serving Christ and his kingdom, long after the national bureaucracy has crumbled.

For the Clergy

Although the clergy cannot, by themselves, bring about a revitalized church, their role is critical. Some needed actions can be taken only by the ordained ministry. Foremost is the need to focus on ways to improve the Sunday morning worship service, particularly the preaching. Laypersons consistently stress the importance of preaching, so it is incredible that the clergy do not give this task top priority. United Methodist pastors have long been aware that mediocre preaching will not jeopardize their careers; after all, neither the bishop nor the district superintendents have more than cursory information on an elder's preaching ability.

Good preaching requires that the preacher believe deeply in his or her message. A life-changing message produces effective messengers. The preacher puts his or her faith on the line whenever a sermon is preached. Good preaching requires not only long and careful preparation, but also the risk of presenting one's faith publicly. Preaching is more difficult than attending committee meetings in the conference headquarters or counseling with individuals—little wonder then that some of our pastors have become distracted from the task of preaching. Nevertheless a pastor does nothing that is more important. It is not an exaggeration to say that the first step toward a revitalized church must begin on Sunday morning.

Changes in the way the denomination does things must be made by the clergy with support from the laity. Some of the needed changes will, at least in the short-term, threaten the clergy. Abolishing the minimum salary, after several decades of annually trying to increase it, is an example. Demanding courageous leaders who will take the church in new directions, instead of managers who maintain the institutional *status quo,* is another. Being willing to trust the laity may be perceived as a challenge to the pastor's position in the local church. Nevertheless we remain convinced that those men and women who have been called by God into the ordained ministry of The United Methodist Church take both their calling and their ordination vows seriously, that they know the essence of their vocation lies in their ability to serve the people of God, rather than in having the people serve the clergy. Most continue to place the needs of the church above personal preferences, even when this requires substantial personal sacrifice and risk.

A unique responsibility of the clergy is to see that high standards for preparation, effectiveness and conduct for United Methodist ministers are maintained. It is the clergy who must determine whether the candidates for ordination are committed to the faith and have the necessary gifts and graces necessary for the ordained ministry. They have the responsibility to see that their peers maintain high standards, including dismissing those who, for whatever reason, fail to be effective.

Finally, the clergy, as well as the laity must realize that the local church is the most important part of the denomination.

Here the gospel is preached. Here people either become Christians or fail to do so. If the local congregations are vital and effective, the whole church prospers. If the local churches are ineffective at winning people to Christ, the elaborate connectional structure is like a house built on sand.

A Final Word

In the final analysis, the church is of God, who calls it to the task of witness and ministry. The heirs of John Wesley have been used of God for over two centuries. The Wesleyan heritage continues to provide an effective basis for our ministry as The United Methodist Church moves into its third century.

While God calls us, we must respond to that call. The decisions United Methodist clergy and laity must make in the period ahead will determine the future course, perhaps even the continued existence, of United Methodism. We are convinced that God is still calling The United Methodist Church to witness and to serve, to "spread scriptural holiness throughout the land." The response is up to us.